My Life, Love, and Limericks

PLAYS BY JOSEPH KESSELRING

Aggie Appleby, Maker of Men (1933)
There's Wisdom in Women (1935)
Cross-Town, (1937)
Arsenic and Old Lace (1941)
Maggie McGilligan (1942)
Identically Yours (1945)
4 Twelves Are 48 (1949)
Surgery Is Indicated (1954)
Accidental Angel (1955)
A Frog in His Pocket (1958)
Bearded Lady with a Kindly Knife (1964)
Mother of That Wisdom (published 1973)

MY LIFE, LOVE, AND LIMERICKS

An Autobiography in Verse by

Joseph Kesselring

Author of *Arsenic and Old Lace*

With an Appreciation by
EDWARD UHLAN

An Exposition-Banner Book

Exposition Press   New York

EXPOSITION PRESS, INC.

50 Jericho Turnpike, Jericho, New York 11753

FIRST EDITION

SBN 0-682-47659-5

Published simultaneously in Canada by Transcanada Books

CONTENTS

AN APPRECIATION

Although our paths had crossed in the literary and theatrical milieux of New York, I was not counted among the fortunate who knew Joseph Kesselring well. I wish I were. Poets have always stood tall among my favorite people. Not that Kesselring had ever earned a reputation as a poet, though he could have had he so chosen. Like others of his untold number of admirers, however, I knew him principally as the playwright who created *Arsenic and Old Lace,* later made into a motion picture, and other Broadway plays. I also knew that he had written a potpourri of short stories and sketches of various sorts, had directed and acted in amateur theatrical productions, was a professional singer during his early career and made the many-faceted cultural pursuits of the metropolis a part of his daily life. Only after his death did I discover that he had been a poet as well.

Yet throughout his life, from the age of eleven, Joseph Kesselring had been a prolific poet. Few days passed that he did not set down his impressions in verse. Even those lines of his boyhood years point to the man and poet he was to become, for he unquestionably had a particular talent for crystallizing his thoughts and emotions in poetic form. The result is a large body of poems, all of them of distinctive quality, some of them superb. His wife and a few of his intimates alone knew of this collection. Every public personality, I suppose, has a private life. Poetry became his, a retreat in which he was the sole occupant, one where he could voice his innermost self to his own satisfaction—not the public's. He stipulated that the poetry not be published during his lifetime.

Now that he is gone, the ban has been lifted. Time has come to share this collection with others. The poems divide themselves

7

into several natural groupings. One slender section provides samplings of his boyhood verse, surprisingly imaginative in its imagery and observation of his youthful world. These stanzas sound the prelude to his autobiographical poems, taking him from adolescence into maturity and late years. Here we see Joseph Kesselring's development both as man and artist. And here—among other choice offerings—are love poems addressed to his wife, commentaries on a European journey, tributes to his friends, Lincoln, and the composer Palestrina (one of his idols), poems of lament, joy, and his faith in God. Many of these poems mirror his faculty to capture the extraordinary in the passing scene, where others saw nothing but the mundane.

Brightening the whole is the poet's wit which, by a deft turn of phrase, transmogrifies seemingly serious lines into high humor. This same humor spontaneously comes to the fore in the diverting group of limericks which the author turned out with an A-B-C ease. Two long poems, "Stranger at the Gate" and "Oh, Blessed Company! A Cocktail Party!" and a sizable compilation of miscellaneous poetry complete the volume.

One cannot leave these poems without reflecting on the richness of the mind that created them. The poet possessed a rare diversity of gifts: keenness of intellect, imagination, flair for the telling word and phrase, an innate *joie de vivre*, artistic integrity, and an overall view that brought these elements together in exactly the right proportions. I consider it a high privilege to share, through his poems, in this endowment. When I began to set these thoughts down, I said I was not well acquainted with Joseph Kesselring. Perhaps I should alter that statement. After reading his poetry, I know the man well, indeed, as a fellow human and, yes, a friend, for poetry is the most intimate—and revealing—of languages. His friendship is one I shall always cherish.

EDWARD UHLAN

BOYHOOD RECOLLECTIONS

GRANDMOTHER'S TEA

At seven or eight years I giggled to see
My grandmother's way with a cup of tea.
She'd hot-up the pot with furious water,
Measure the leaves like a mandarin's daughter,
Drop them precisely by tilting the spoon,
Then pour in the fury!—while I, like a loon,
Snickered the mirth of a strap-worthy brat:
"How silly, for *tea*, a performance like that!"
And while it was steeping—(just *so* long, *that* rite:
"It *must* be cooked, Grandma!" . . . "Not yet, dear, not quite.
Good tea should be, oh, strong! a really dark amber.
Weak tea is so—passive!—no presence, no timbre!")
And *while* it was "*cooking*" she'd set the tea trappings;
The sugar, and pound cake—(I *would* lick its wrappings)
And *milk*—"*Never* cream, dear! The thought brings my *quease*
  up!"—
And spoon, knife and napkin—and—Grandma's own *teacup*!
Grandmother's teacup was fragile and pink;
Completely too small for an adequate drink.
(I snortled to mind—though her hand *was* real wee—
How I drank from *buckets*, and quite easily!)
She once had a dozen. *Her* grandmother bought them
In England, and when she "came over" she brought them.
"A journey of months, dear, the boat was so slow."
I got the impression her gramps had to *row*.
The other cups? "Dear me!—you know your grandfather.
He *won't* dry things gently. He thinks it's a bother.
It's not that he drops them; his hands are like wrenches.
He *squeezes* them! Mercy! You'd think they were wenches!
But I'd part with the cups that he's crumbled me out of,
To banish that *monster* he drinks *his* tea out of!
He won it at quoits, you know, Champion's Trophy,
And I *could* stand its color and size, though they're oafy,
But it's shaped *so* much like—! Oh, embarrassingly!

11

And to use *such* a vessel for tea! *Mercy me*! . . .
But dear—don't repeat it.". . . . (She smiled. I felt odd.)
He's trying at times but—he isn't *quite* God."
Yes, Grandpa drank tea, too— as green as a gremlin,
And strong as old mule water aged in the Kremlin.
The leaves in *his* pot he boiled over and over:
My old papa-gramps learned the trick back in Dover!
You get *all* the taste of the tea if you boil it.
And don't add too *much* fresh, or dammit, you'll spoil it!"
I felt that my gramps was a *man,* men *among!*
(He died with the whispered word "love" on his tongue.)
Grandmother held her cup small-pinky-hidden.
To show it, she said, was most strictly forbidden.
I wondered. I'd seen the rich Mrs. Van Dorn
With pinky thrust out from her cup like a horn.
"Well, riches and rightness don't always team up.
See, dear: *cream* is rich but not right in a cup
That's waiting for milk that is just right for tea.
But then, people rich can be right too, you see."
I didn't. "But, Grandma," I said. "Look, the *tea*!
I mean—well, it's only just water and—gee!
You cook in those crumbs and—well, honest, *I* think it
Just tastes *awful* funny! So why do you drink it?"
"Well, Grandson—" She paused. "Oh, then, all right, here's
    why:
I was *holding* a cup when I caught Grandpa's eye." . . .
"When he *first* saw you?" . . . "Yes. Oh, I'll *never* forget!
My heart went ker-plump! I can feel the thump yet!
I sat drinking tea with his two Boston aunties.
Such ladies they were. You could see their lace panties! . . .
Oh, no, dear!—down low, dear!—just up from their boots!
They served *Chinese* tea and thin biscuits and fruits.
And then, dear—your Grandpa came in . . ." Grandma sighed.
"He stood there—so handsome—so tall and so wide.
We met—and he told me—(I wore a lace dress)
I looked like a fairy-book royal princess!
And that's *why,* you see, dear. At tea I'm my best.

And you'll notice, at *tea,* dear, I'm always *quite* dressed."
Then she picked up her spoon—the soft-shiny gold one—
And *was JUST* a princess!—though maybe an old one.
But *I* was a small *mule:* "But *Grandma!*—the *tea!*
"You *can't LIKE* to drink it! It looks just like—'*wee*'!"
Grandma sat still—smiled. "Lean closer, dear—do. . . .
Don't *ever* tell Grandpa! . . . *I* think it does, *too!*"

So I Would Have Written

"I shall *not* go out into
The garden and eat worms!
I shall *not* take my ball
And go home!—so there, so *there*!"

"Because, because, my common
Sense says that worms breed germs
In boys, and because I do not
Want the ball! *I—do—not—CARE*!"

So I thought, and would have
written long ago. . . .
What can you write at six?—
When you do not know

How to write, *how* to express
The deep of tragedy?—
When only sick-loss fills you,
Says "why, why?" Asks "is it me?"—

When love, and to be wanted,
Needed, to be essential
To those essential ones,
By lack is brand-burned "nonessential"!

A Gate I Loved

As a lad I stubbed my toe on
   a large, dry bone.
   I hated that bone.
I threw it at a poor old gate I *loved*—
   A squeaky gate, a *weak* old gate . . . .
   The gate fell . . . .
   My hate fell.
The gate and my hate both died.
The gate and my hate both fell on *me*—
   And *I* fell—
   And I cried.

The Chestnut Tree

At age nine he first met the chestnut tree
Older by 30-odd years than he.
It stood alone by a dry-rock wall.
(He thought that God must be *just* that tall.)
He felt its trunk with hands as knowing
As the bark that told him of its growing.
He climbed its limbs and found its fruit,
Tearing the cloth of his Sunday Suit.
He lay on its roots in its sun-warmed shade
And gazed through its leaves and unknowingly prayed
That he, tree and everything *please* would remain
Just *this* way forever and ever, Amen.

Remorse

How frightful that a boy of ten
Should harm a harmless creature when
In after years he'd give an arm
If he could just undo the harm.
The bird!—the kitten!—dying, *dead!*
The rabbit! *No!—the way it bled!*
Great God of Love!—we *can't* repair?
Why can't we? Don't *You* feel?—or *care?*
No—no. . . . *I* know. . . . Time gone is gone.
And *life* in that time—gone, gone, *gone!*
And as we fouled Compassion's name
We *pay*—now—in remorse and shame.

As a Boy I Leaped

As a boy I leaped, on a warm, dry day,
From a barn beam into a mow of hay.
It was odd how I didn't land at all,
Just sank like a puff till I ceased to fall.
Of course, I was nine years of just bones and skin,
And the fodder was fresh cut and loosely tossed in,
So I lay for a breath in my rustling crevasse,
Simply living forever so time couldn't pass.
(Though I hadn't a notion that time shouldn't pass.)
And my nose sniffled in the fresh flavor of hay
And I sneezed and recovered and wriggled and lay

In my spongily fragrant and whispering grasses,
Too young to know that all ecstasy passes.
(It's quite true, I'm sure, that there's somewhere a Master
That chooses to save certain boys from disaster.
You label Him "Destiny"?—"Fate"? If you'll pardon,
I *know* He's the single old God of "The Garden"!)
For I flung out my arms, and swept them around,
And buried them under my backbone . . . and found
That, hard, cold and sharp, on its stem of wood,
Rigidly upright, a pitchfork stood!

WHAT WONDERFUL ELSE?

What wonderful else can a small farm yield
To a boy of twelve, like a tall corn field?
To be lost there, deep in, and nobody dreaming
He's lost there, deep in, and the corn feathers streaming
An arm overhead—so that time wanders on
And nobody knows where the "poor boy's" gone.

Oh, they're sorry, so sorry they've treated him poorly,
And shortly they'll search for him, shortly, and surely
They'll weep when he's missing and speak of him kindly—!
But oh, he'll be staggering, painfully, blindly,
Lost in the wilderness, trapped in the rows,
Going through agonies nobody knows! . . .

Lost in the corn field—ten yards from people!
And oh, darn it all, quite in sight of a steeple!

Untitled Poem

My soul is like a fallen leaf, lifeless, withered, dry,
My heart a land where sorrow reigns chief,
      where all that is glad must die.
My spirit like a fire by water deluged,
      lies blackened, unfeeling, dead,
Like a battlefield daisy by a man's blood rouged,
      bows down its desecrated head.

Written at age 11.
Dictated to Charlotte Kesselring
by Joseph Kesselring, July 9, 1967.

WILLOW HILL

OUR HOUSE

We bought the place because the mountain faced it.
Because the floors were clean, and fragrance graced it.

ON THIS HILL

Here on this hill there is *Life*: things of forever,
Rock, dirt and flower, all forever things,
Tree, bird and light—and *us*, we two and breath;
All loved and that loves! You know? See! Destroy
Every atom of this hill, earth, *all* that is here,
And for us—nothing, nothing would disappear!

WORDS TO A CHILD

Don't step on it, darling! Not *that* one! The rug
Would *curl* at the death of a true Ladybug.

Ladybugs, dear, are the nicest of people,
they're most of them born in a church, in the *steeple!*
They never bite, never! They don't even sting!
And they smell just as nice as a candy-box string.
And *clean*, darling?—*clean?* They're as fine-polished clean
as the gold of a cross, or a pod-covered bean.

Don't step on them ever, dear. Ladybugs cry.
And, stepped on, they bleed and—of course, dear—they die.

EVEN A BUG

You know?—*you* know what it is?—
　　You know what it *is* to *need*
　　　　something to *love*?—something
　　　　　alive, to make *happy*?
You *do*?
Then find *anything* alive
　　that needs you—
　　　　and *love* it.
Even a mouse.
Even a *bug!*

GRIEF

My own little darling stood
　　　　and cried
Because her thumb-planted rose
　　　　had died.

BLESS LIFE!

The tiny bug drops into my mug
　　　　of warm honey-milk.
But oh—bless Life!—the poor thing
　　　　drops in only to share!—
And finds death in it. While I find
　　　　just some hours' sleep.
So—bless Life!—if it fouls it
　　　　minutely, should I care?

MARCH DOUBTING

That green bit there on the ground fairly
      leaps at me.
I sit here with the icy soil beneath my
      frigid ass.
The month is March. And I, bone-chilled
      to scepticism,
Cold-stupid, *can't* believe that bit of
      green is grass.

But it is, you know! I leaned and touched
      and plucked a shoot—
And crushed and pressed it to my frosty-
      doubting snoot.
It's grass, all right, and I feel better—
      good—*great!*—and
      warm, to boot.

THE CHEST

The chest, sill-high, hammered—
      You'd swear it was gold.
It's brass, massive, glint-lit
      and lovely, and old.
Time knows its first home-place,
      its maker. It should
hold grand ancient treasure—
      it holds fire-wood.

Song to an Apple-log Fire

Who knows the first-time sprouting, fruiting of the apple tree?—
Tree that in some time-drowned past found, sunning on its limbs,
Rose-enveloped meat of fruit that housed—how many seeds?—
Of apple; that sired the "sinning" of first-flesh ecstasy,
Of *that* coy pair, of us, of all the potent "hers" and "hims"
From then till now! (*If* you believe in serpent-counseled deeds.)

Magical design? Accident? What marked the apple tree?
Fruit alone, blossom, beauty of leaf and form are not above
All other trees. And surely "he" would have cared to munch
A peach, a fig, a plum!—sweet citrus!—and why not a cherry?
And were there not berries, if fruit's the point? And even "she,"
    with love,
Would have ground, pulped, in her new-toothed head, nut meats!
    —*good* "crunch"!

Always the apple. "Comfort me with apples!" And that man,
That "Johnny" man, his fool-blessed, heavy bag of apple seed,
His trudging, lug-seed journey: Why not pear, the muley bump-
    kin?
And am I the first to wonder?—mock hero "Tell," the bowman,
    who began
The witless practice: shooting of an arrow at—(I doubt the
    need)—
An *apple* on an urchin's head? ("Nothing," *I'd* have snarled, "if
    not a pumpkin!")

Apple, apple! "Sauce" I'm offered, "—jack," the liquid buy,

"Baldwin," "Snow" and "Johnathan" in form of juicy "raw"!
Told am I my teeth will gleam and flash, and palate water
At bite of apple! And bless the soul, in pie?—it's in the sky!
So I'm told: the *only* fruit with scrapple, pork—with moldy *straw!*
Take *daily* apple! *God* will feed the doctor's wife and daughter!

Well, well! Then how forced am I to give my heart to apple tree!
For I have lounged, some blissful hours now, before a fireplace,
Before logs on the grate, before *that* wood in best flame's duty:
Pink-rose-pink it is, whispering, and gentlewarm upon my knee.
So! Can I besnoot what power commands this apple grace?—
That, dancing, offers *all* of bone-felt, flaming beauty?

I love the early morning light
　　that frosts the lawn.
Rise early, catch it quick,
　　or it is gone.
What? September holds no *frost*?—
　　it is warmly kind?
Oh, pooh! Illusion is the color
　　of the mind!

A Simple Thing

I think I'll write a simple thing
That calls for only pulse to sing
Of sea and bird and wind and me—
And rhythm of eternity.

P.S.—A Further Thought

I thought to write of simple things,
Of lily leaves and package strings,
Of travel trunk and Christmas tree—
And all I wrote about—was *me!*—

To Nancy—Christmas 1946

Dear Nancy:
Just fancy!
A real little kitten named Fiddle K.
Told us the day before yesterday,
That for Christmas you didn't want cheese cake
                    or mittens,
But you *would* like a nice little book about kittens.
So here is the book, from both Fiddle and us.
We hope that you have a real
                    Merry Christ*mus!*

Charlotte, Joseph and Fiddle Kesselring

26

To Louane—Christmas 1946

Dear Oulane:
We'd like to make it plain
That this is a live frog.
He was sound asleep in the bog
Under a rock in our pool.
You know, frogs do this as a rule.
Some people call it "hibernation":
But take my word for it, the explanation
Has nothing to do with the nation of "Hibers."
There's no such thing: they're just the fibers
Of somebody's cockeyed imagination.
Somebody like "Resselking," whose literary station
Was attained by writing fairy tales,
You know, about snakes and snails and wafflesnogs and things?
Anyway, Charlotte and I just want to say,
This live frog is sleeping in your sock,
So you'll know it's Christmas without looking at the clock.

M
  E
    R
      R
        Y
          −C
            H
              R
                I
                  S
                    T
                      M
                        A
                          S

Charlotte and Joseph K.

THE BOY GROWS OLDER*

(Grandmother sat with her tatting.)

Of *course,* dear, you love her deeply!—and *her* loved ones!—but,
    a *cat?*
Well, now! If love adds weight you have enough to make you fat!
But don't be fooled that love for this one, that one, or a kitty
Matters less for love divided so; or that it's pity
That kitty shares the same love as *God*-like fashioned loved one.
Love is love is love is love! But you'll think I'm making fun.

(She dropped her work, an edging on some lace.)

Real love, dear—oh, you can't degree it! But it's not a *mood,*
    disjointed;
It's *never* warped by whim, or transient fancy—*or* annointed
By God for special delivery! . . . Here, I'll tell you, dear! *Real*
    love *seeks* a word
Of *need* for it. That's it!—and never dies; but just—when *we* go—
    breathes *unheard.*

(Grandma went on with her tatting.)

---

*With a titular bow to the great, late Heywood Broun.

28

OH, SING OF LOVE

Oh, sing of love for three!—great, healthy, saving love for three!

She loves her God, she loves her man, and she loves her cat.
She does love them, does love them thus in the order that
You read them here—if, blest, you read them. And it's twelve to
  seven
This love will see all of them, together, walking Heaven!

*So sing of love's degree BEYOND great, healthy, saving love for
  three!*

TO "FIDDLE"

I knew a cat, yes, and a cat knew me.
We found fine love together, and mutual felicity.
We traveled, ate and slept together, quite around the map.
And of all sweet rests, she loved the best my darling's loving lap.
God give me heaven, oh, just the ultimate grace
To see the long-haired cat and my darling's dear face!
God grant me heaven,—please God, *God!*—that satin head,
That deep-purring love, beneath my reaching hand, beneath
  my darling's bed.

A little "lap" is a lovely thing
It makes the heart of a kitty sing.
It's grand, it's great, it's simply swell!
Oh, much too sweet for purrs to tell!

To the "Girls"

Blitz and Piccle,*
Piccle and Blitz:
Two cats sitting as Buddha sits.
Blitz and Piccle,
Piccle and Blitz,
Wise-thanking Buddha
For kittenish wits!

"Lovey," I heard the bird say to the cat,
"Long, long ago, it was told to us that
"We should love one another."

---

*Piccle pronounced Peekle.

Hail to the Feline!

Last night I wrote a piece of worth.
It dealt with things of life:
Mosquitoes, mice and rats—
Creatures: dogs and cats.
Today I read it over, with my wife:
It says that cats and cats and cats
Shall—I vow—inherit the earth.
And—do you know?—I *swear!*—
I believe this thing.
The cat—immaculate, sufficient—
Will be king!

The Cry of a Fly

Now think—now *think*—if *you* were a fly,
Given wings and the freedom by nature to *fly,*
Would you not find it distressing to die,
Simply because you were born as a fly?

Lovely Enemy

The dawn can be a sneak. Oh, yes, it can!
You're up at night; you hadn't planned for *all* night.
You've worked late; but just *late*. It *can't* be *six!*
Yet creeping gray, then blue; then rich gold-red sneak-tints
The sash, the room and you like rude intruder
With reproof on ketchup-tongue and hectic-healthy cheek.
Oh, damn! It's six, all right; the neighbor's dog is out—
The neighbor, too!—whistling!—*shouting!*—the noisy lout!
But come, come!—the day *is* prime for rested things, no doubt.
But not for you, no, not. For you it's pen rout,
A lovely enemy you'd like to do without.

A Willow Tree

No tree is like a willow tree
That weeps in drooping jollity,
That mocks its dirge of mournful fall
By chuckling underneath its pall.

You think a willow's really sad?
You think it thinks its time is bad?—
Its time and all that lives around it?
I don't. I've touched one and I found it
Quite a trunk of rustling laughter,
Touched one during grief and after,

Pressed myself against its bark,
Shared its outlook on our park,
Shared its view through sad-hung leaves,
Learned no willow ever grieves.

THE OTHER BOTTLE

How carefully she hid the other bottle!

You don't assassinate the maid, or throttle
Your pawkey aunt because she prompts the silly
Maid—(how I dislike that maid, the lard-assed filly!)—
To seize and cart and hide away the sherry
In places you would hesitate to bury
A poor wee mouse, a horse, a dinosaur!

That milk-eyed maid finds hollows for the drink that, *cor!*—
An undertaker's staff would be at bad odds
To find the hidings!

        Well, I have my gods—
I have them all!—who seat themselves upon my nose
And lead me to the grove that Bacchus chose!

Not Quite Right?

I'm slightly puzzled. See: just now
I *thanked* a lady with a bow.
She answered sweetly, pleasantly:
"You're much obliged!" she said to me.

I may be wrong, I'm not so bright.
But something there seems not quite right.

Deny the Dark

When we, that night, were covered with a sky
So black that coal was quivering jealously,
(We *felt* the quivering of our bin of coal!)
I said we should *deny* the dark—at least try
To make *light* of sightlessness. Then I said, "Why
Should *we* complain of simple loss of seeing, we
Who have—well—fire, light *within*, to spot our goal?"

But you: "Dear! *Please!* The moon *is* gone and stars are gone!
Your fancy talk! *Here*, on our *terrace!*—our *own!*—
We, you and I, our shapes, our—well, our *us-ness!* Gone!"

I laughed. "Great honest-injun, dear!—the stars will be again;
and *we!*
And you will look at me and I at you, and we will see."

Triple Meal

I squat by the glassy pond—still.
    I watch a hungry carp.
It rises. Its planned meal, a frog,
    goes "plunk" like a rusty harp
And gulps a fly—and is gulped! A
    fox trots down (Do *I* sit here?)
To dart, snap and snatch his triple
    meal!—wheel, race and disappear.

I stir, sorry that fox and carp and
    frog and human *I*
Must prey so eagerly, must feed as we
    can, or life will die.

Not Always Golden

My girl is in the kitchen rinsing towels.
I like the sound—her business in rinsing.
Odd, to feel a lively liking for a noise.
For it *is* noise. Of course it's noise! What else?

Yes. But damn the moment if-when the noise is not!
If-when silence, shrieking, holds me where I sit!

He Shall Have Music

Last night my girl snored like a working saw.
Unusual! Nine hundred nights but one
She sleeps noiseless as a healthy mouse.
(We have a cat that sleeps more noisily.)

Annoyance *may* have swept the ceiling—
How should *I* know?—I, lulled to sleep
By the music of a working saw.

How Lucky the Jay

Every clear morning at early o'clock
All of the jays in the county flock
Into the field below our dwelling,
Shriek themselves hoarse; such raucus yelling
Seldom you've heard; and so without reason.
(It's now well past the mating season.)
While robin and chickadee try, through the din,
To warble the morning decently in.

How lucky the jay is so damned handsome.
The rest of him's worth a bedbug's ransom!

To Chickadee

You chickadee!—you pertly brave bewingéd mite!
I sit here watching you. It's early, barely light.
I'm awed. You're so minute and yet you, shrieking, fight
The bigger birds for food and wing room! Just the sight
Of common birdseed, much less the massive bite
In giant shell like sunflower, damps the fright
You surely feel for birds whose monstrous size quite
Pee-weed you. . . . Good living, chickadee!—fat rib and healthy
     feather
To take you through the bitter winter you must weather.

Field of Returning

We have a hill-field that looks down on a valley.
(Up the lane and through the gap; turn to the left a bit.)
It's cold now, and still; winter holds it till tomorrow.
Then the sun will warm it, home-come birds call to birds,
Creatures tune their creaky pipes in new-green fragrance.

And we will go to it, lie on it, and feel its new life
Rich beneath our backs; lie on it flat, *taking* the sun.
And when we do that we'll know again that in *this* life
We've found a haven that will live beyond our breathing,
A place to *meet* beyond this breath, beyond this life;
This-*our* place, our field of meeting, of returning.

Words for van Wagners

For "Mamie"

There was the grandfather and the father and the three sons.
I knew them all and, by my life, they were all of them men.
Three still live and, did my life depend upon their hands,
I'd toss my *life* into their hands, abruptly, knowing that I would
  live.

He walked in a lonely valley, a distant shadow-held place.
There was no sight, no sound, no smell of familiar comfort.
He knew he lived in a waking dream of all that was strange and
  wrong.
And then he stumbled 'round a bend in a tangled path—
And tripped on a sun-struck rock, warm, with a warmth he knew,
And prostrate, he wept, and waked—and felt that love had found
  him.

MY FRIEND

The man who was the father of my wife,
Who walked and talked and drank with me,
Who spoke of decency and patience,
Who turned in anger on a crude intruder . . .

This man is dead.

I ask that when I, too, am dead
I may be permitted the company of this man.

Hope, *hope,* that black window gleam kindly at night,
hearth fire give more than dull, smoke-twisted light—
that waterfall, shrill-falling—*close*—in the park!—
be turned to sweet music, soft-borne by the dark.

Hope, hope, *more* than hope that a *kind* dark will bring
compassion of nature to chase fearful thing.

CERTAINTY

How fortunate the one, who, when his time comes to die,
Dies in a familiar place.
But more—how fortunate the one who, knowing the last breath,
Surely—through an uncertain eye—
Sees love on a beloved face.

Heaven *must* hold that such a dying could not, could
Not be hard or frightening,
Could be only a gentle-certain rolling over the line into certainty;
A rolling eased by love, love that is nothing of darkness or dread,
Love that gently, gently tells that nothing, nothing dies or is
   dead,
Speaks nothing of darkness, that is only all of constant light—
   enlightening.

WHEN I'M DEAD

I want, when I'm dead, only the *contained* mourning
Of those who have loved me.
I want, now, to know that, when I'm gone.
No *hopeless* grief will disturb me.
And surely this wish, in life, will hold beyond life—
Give me reason to disapprove of grief that is beyond hope,
Grief that has no touch with life existing here, there, anywhere.
I want, when I'm dead, only the continued love
Of those who have loved me.
I want, when I'm dead, only the hope that those whom I love
Will live in a hope to be with me.

What a man is Kesselring,
Former jump and wrestle king.
Now he trips on hill of mole
Grappling with a feather stole.

42

A Straight Line Is Not

He left his gate like a stricken thing.
The road ran straight as a banjo string.
He walked away and away till late. . . .
Then stopped—and smiled—and opened his gate.

Prayer

Now I lay me down in fear,
Dear God, love away my tear.
Dear God, give me inner light
Now I lay me down in fright.

When I lay me down in death,
Dear God, keep me in your breath.

My Own You

Oh, you, my own you!
  While I'm touched with your grace
  I'll never be lost in a frightening place!

Oh, you, my own you!
  While I'm part of your breath
  I'll never be lost in continual death!

LOVE POEMS

DE PROFUNDIS

"De Profundis"? All things are relative.

So, *from* the depths, to this bliss,
None but the most evil tongue
Could call this vaulting happenstance, *pure* chance.

There were two of us with nothing,
Two with *nothing,* two who starved
And hoped and strove together;
Two who walked in storm, in shoe-soaked leather,
Two who dined on simple gruel,
Two who knew a sharp door knock as cruel
Demand to leave our shelter.
Two who now, through faith, have found
That now, not anyone can knock a sound
Demanding that we leave our place.

There are two of us, in this unbleached security—
Two of us—

My dear, will you believe that I love you?
Can you dismiss my weaknesses?
Oh, my love, I am a vessel with cracks that
                    seem to spew
The devastating evidence of my unworthiness.
But trust me, I believe in and am faithful to
The secret thing we have together.
We began with this; we clutched each other.
                    What grew
With breath, yours and mine mingled?—Surely
                    you knew, and I knew,
In that street, that road, that place, our
                    bond acre—
Surely you know now, as you knew then, that
                    the true
Rigid line of our lives, Yours and mine,
                    as one line—
Oh, wait! Please:—never mind the evidence that
                    would seem superficially to
Damn my word! My dear, my ever and ultimate darling
You are of my heart and soul and body, and I am
                    of yours! I am of *you!*

LOVE

Love is a light
when fright
at night
creeps out of darkness.

MY PRESENT!

Tonight I've a present for one
Whose love might be God's gift of Sun.
I'll lay in her hand every kill-thing,
I'll lay in her hand every gun!—
For this one I love is unwilling
That man should have power of killing.
For this one I love holds my hand,
And I love what her God laws command.
For this one I love—I shall *not* give her *fear!*
No, never! Not *ever!* God *hear* me! God *hear!*

Our Love

I'll keep the love that's been always mine.
    And mine?—
She'll keep my love—for the endless all
    of time!

Something Past?

How easy to speak of love as something past,
As something in the silly-distant years.
But what will we think of in that conscious last?
Will we snicker-laff? or find ourselves in tears?
What we *will* think of is in the depth of heart:
Separated?—gone as two?—or as not at all apart?

Truth of Love

The truth of love lies in something more
than "Bed, bed, *bed*, that's the thing for fun!"
What's left when bed is soiled and parts are sore?
What's left when flesh and bed become a bore?
Is there a *person* left, a *friend?*—a wanted one?
Say "yes, yes!—and *yes*" and there's the one you love in true.
And praise the holy happiness you hold, if *she* loves *you!*

To Her

Her eyes? God colored them with mystic light
      From midnight skies.
Yet were they pale as ice and knew not sight
      I'd love her eyes.

Her lips? Ah, like twin petals of a rose
      Blood-red that drips
The sweetest dew. Yet were they gray, God knows
      I'd love her lips.

Her hair? It is as soft as silk and fine
      As angels wear.
Yet I'd not care and it resembled twine
      I'd love her hair.

Her form? See proud perfection start and turn
      With envy warm.
Yet were she plump and round as any urn
      I'd love her form.

Her soul? God loved it so he called it His
      Eternal goal.
And this of her I love for what it is.
      I love her soul.

My Face

Without her?—there'd have been dead time of failure, but she
  lifted me.
Without her?—all times of failure, so many, she believed in me.
Without her?—well, I live and love and try to chuckle at disgrace
But *not* without her. And *with* her? I live and love,
And love and live and write and hope, and *with* her—keep my
  face!

There Is no End

There is no end—
Love is life—
Love is eternal.

My love is a plant in the heart of me
Thrusting its topmost branches to the sky.
See how the little, green leaves laugh in Heaven.

She is the lovely light that burns
so much more rightly (more, *more* brightly!)
than the poor bewildered flame that found
itself at both ends of a warm-teared waxy thing.

How?

How can one, out of the depth
      of depression,
Be so near to the ecstasy
      of appreciation,
Of beauty—on and between
      the mountains?

How can one be so dark-minded
      and yet feel
The lightness of bright and living love
      for another?
How can one know desolation, and yet still know
      that God *is* love?

I admit, if I could truly speak lightly of the power of love,
I would damn love, and phrase it as a delusion of passion.
But—what if I must, in my experience, swear to what I know of
love—
What if I *must* then say of love, that, for me it is all that I have
known of compassion.

The Truant Heart

When I have spun life's swift, uncertain reel,
Played out its slender cord to the frayed end,
Smiling I'll drop into the void, nor feel
Sorrow nor sense of fear as I descend.
Oh, I love life, the good, rich living of it,
Tall trees, damp grass, keen daylight, sombre night
I love; all, all the dear, live things I quit
With breath and sight and red-blood life and light.
Death is a fat gray hand, ice-cold and wet
With loathsome moisture from the grave. It draws
The blood in terror from my feet. And yet
My coward's soul will laugh at death because
One thing I know—The truant heart of me,
Safe in thy breast, will beat eternally.

SOME DAY

Some day your voice will come to me
   From 'cross those poor, dead years,
And I will turn, so pale, to see
   Them bridged by my own tears.

And you will cross and come to me,
   All bathed in fire and light.
And we will walk in ecstasy
   Down, down into the night.

My girl means so well by me, in telling me to go to bed,
But if I go to bed I *may* sleep, and I may *not*, and *may* be filled
   by silly dread
Of nothing tangible, of nothing really in the night that brings
   me fear,
Nothing that really bothers me—so long as she is near.

No normal one who has the true love of any other being
Will end his own life, or work to bring harm to himself.
Those who take suicide or any lesser form of self destruction
Are unloved, truly unloved, (be they normal in the head).
The love of others for ourselves is the bolt, the anchor
That holds us to life, to healthy life. The thought of the agony!
To her, to him, who would be desolated by our going.
So we are held to life and health, not by our strength,
But by the strength of *love!*—Love for us! The need for us!—
By the realization that our dying would bring desolation
To others—to that other.—We would not *live* alone!

AGAIN, THE ONE I LOVE

Oh, I know I write so much about the one I love, who loves *me.*
And sure I know that repetition is the father of monotony.
But where's the lad who loves, and knows he's loved in spite of
him,
Who spares his pen, or tongue, or fist to illustrate the right of
him?

There's a place where I live,
a peace place,
apart,
Where nothing is heard
but a rhythm—
her heart.

THAT PERSON

I had a little quarrel with that person.
And, ever since, I've studied, been rehearsin'
How I'd vaunt myself to flaunt my crest.
But now—she smiled at me! And *face* it!—
I feel *blessed!*

To stay together, man and wife, for life?—
Is this the cutting of an ill-edged knife?
No! carving *to* you, the one you want for ever:
First you must decide that you could leave her—*never!*

Love? Is this the thing that hones all of life
Into something sharper than a blade, a razor knife?
Love? Is this the thing that gently turns the soul
Into something sweeter than pure honey's goal?
Why question? True love—yes, true—fulfills all bliss.
You doubt? Give yourself to a loved one's loving kiss.

I *love* her?—for reason *unknown* to me?
Pah! I love her for *being*, for loving *me;* and see:
I love her for the reason that I love *her*, just one:
For is she not my darkness, and my sun?

Why is it that the things I write
seem dull to me, seem poor
until my girl, with her voice,
that voice, reads them to me?
With that voice she covers them,
anoints them, *oils* them
So that my writing seems far more,
far better than the words,
the phrases scratched by my *lead* pencil.
Why is it? Can love strike out,
fix, glorify the common phrases
pressed to a pad, spilled from
a mind dependent upon a grace
of love—to soak them in beauty?

LOVE MUST LIKE

Love and Like are twin-alike,
        as strangers they are *not*.
For Love must wait for Like to strike,
        and Like's of Love begot.

Truth of Love

To quarrel with the one you love
Is not
The slightest evidence of a love
Forgot.

Forgive Presumption

A little girl is a creature so divine
I wish that all, *all* little girls were mine!
Forgive presumption, God!—*But* if they all were mine,
I'd give my heart to keep them so divine.

One little girl, (she *was* a little girl) remained divine.
And by *her* will, and *mine,* and *God's,* she became mine.
And all so many years have gone, and still she's mine.
And I'm hers, still, so much of hers—because she's mine.

The Youngest Love

Old love is the youngest love.
In miles-deep certainty it knows
that Love's *own* love—
(the final blending of all worths,
the ever-two-souls-one)
—has just begun
when hoarse, romantic word
and coarse, sex-muscled gesture
have lost necessity.

A Grown-Child's Prayer

Love is the absence of darkness,
And darkness the absence of light.
I pray let the sun shine today, God,
And give her a candle tonight.

My Little Bo-Peep
will always keep
her sheep—
by Grace of God—
through me.

My Little Bo-Peep,
with love so deep,
will always keep
the Grace of God—
for me.

61

The boy reached out for the little girl—
And she knew he loved her.
And she was right.
She trembled. . . . And he said:
      "We should go home now.
      Your mother will be
         looking for you."
And they went home.

Years later:
The boy reached out for the girl.
And she knew he loved her,
And she was right.
          He trembled—
And she was his—
And *has* been, through all
Those years till now.

Most voice of poetry has spoken love,
And spoken so superbly, that my voice
brain-hesitates to speak of all
that *I* have found in love, that *we* have found
in everything that's bound us in a force of love,
that strips us of the power to write
or speak of *love* beyond the power of expression!
Oh, but we *must* say—simply—we *will* love, beyond breath!
We *do* love!—*will* love!—unnumbered thousand years that follow
 death!

A Man Speaks

Late as it is, (and my darling says it's three)
I feel that I should speak this last word for ecstasy:
"Love is all selflessness, desire, and a dread of losing her,
And a knowing that her heaven is in your choosing her."

Two Lines

Two lines I wrote to my beloved.
God helped me.
And I could write, and write,
And write for all my span, and
Not make known so truly well
The love I hold for her, the love
The love I hold for her, today,
Tomorrow and tomorrow and forever—
Without God's help.

Well, now, how shall I speak of her?
Shall I say that she is brave and gay?
Yes, I can speak of her in this way.
Shall I say that she is beautiful and strong?
Yes, she is that. Shall I say she will belong
To *me*?—of her own and only her decision?
Yes! She is a lady of adorable precision,
Shall I say that *I* love her? I *do*, I *do!*
Shall I say that *she* loves *me. She* said, "It's true!"
Well, then!—I find I am *loved* by, and *I* love a saint!
And if, by *God's word* it's disputed! Well, it aint!

The girl, the woman
    holds me—
Grants my well-meant efforts—
    scolds me.
The girl, the woman—
    please!—in *after*—
Let me know her frown—
    and laughter.

64

PRAYER

I ask genius, so that
I may *speak* my love.
Please! I pray
Give me something more than
This feeble talent—
That I may!

OLD WORDS OF A BEARDLESS GRAYBEARD

I love, I love, I've loved through slow-rapid years.
I love, I loved when love washed out small-silly tears.
I love, I love her-mayhap-here-love now.
I love, I love when nervous love has formed dear-wrinkled brow.
I loved her so, ago, when our then-love creeped
across a rancid-muddy ditch it should have leaped!
I love—I love her as the leaf must love the tree—
Because—Oh bless!—I *love* her!—yes!—as *she*—I *know*—loves *me*!

One Voice

So lonely, so dismally lonely,
Alone in the absence of light.
Yes, fear-struck, heart-bloodlessly lonely,
Alone in the darkness of night,
Alone in the love-empty night.

One body and touch meaning light,
One voice that said, "Lonely? Not lonely!
Together we breathe, and chase night,
Together we've not heard of fright!" . . .
But you're gone! And I'm frightened!—and lonely!—

POEMS OF ITALY

AGO, TO THAT TEMPLE

Ago, to that temple of ancient Sibylla,
A proud Latin laddie rode far for to kneel a
Most humble, beseeching and linen-spared knee;
To ask if he should or, sweet please!—*shouldn't* he
Seek fortune and speak to "her" parents, or no?—
And how about fighting in Gaul? Should he go?

And merciful gods!—should a Roman, oh, ever,
Acknowledge a child by a Greek slave?—or never?
And should he or shouldn't he, must he or not
Acknowledge so much more that should be forgot?

"Dear Sibyl," he brayed, "read the guts of that hen
And kindly please state what I *should,* and, please, *when!*—
Or state that I shouldn't! And cause me to swear
That I won't and I won't and she *can't* make me care!"

"By blade and by blood and hot liver of fowl,
Walk blindly to FLESH at the hoot of an owl!
Go home now—on FOOT!" . . .
                                        He *went* home. . . .

                                                          And me?
Today I full stepped him in *my* century,
And tried to see Sibyl—and hoped she'd see me,
And hoped she had helped *him.* And might—please!—help *me?*

Just Water

It was just water, in a large, wet way,
A monstrous brimming cup of worthy water.
Then, soft-bright, from a straw-gold shore, a *light*
Oil-swept the surface and bounced!—to me!—you!
A color beyond word to say: that *blue!*
And just water!—of the Mediterranean!

"By any Other Name"

Often I'm struck, in Old World, by the presence
Of million-many people named as "peasants."
I live in doubt about the meaning of the term.
(I've heard it spoken as another word for "worm"!)
That was a "peasant"? But he fashions copper urns!—
Taps and graves and bends and taps until he turns
Unruly metal into sculptured loveliness!
Well!—so then, no doubt, the name's a thing to bless!
For sure it must be wonderfully pleasant
To be a "peasant" as Cellini was a "peasant"!

SWALLOWS IN ROME

In Rome a thousand swallows fly
Almost into your room, and cry
The ancient swallow cry in Rome,
Unknowing they're in Caesar's home.

Unknowing? But they're Caesar's dust!
Then sure they flew as now they must
Flick past the temple, catching flies,
Breathing of Caesar, catching flies,
Catching flies like a swallow's father!

Have they a feeling that they'd rather
Eat the flies of a swallow's father
Simply because some ancient father
Flew for a fly in ancient Rome?
Flies are flies in a swallow's home.

Pantheon Cats

Ah, the poor sick Pantheon cats, so lost,
Tossed to the mercies of anyone's whim!
Give *naught* for *naught*, God!—and to *him* the *most*
For his fleetingest pity for kitty! To him
Of nothing of slightest compassion for cat,
Give him a blow of catastrophe's fist,
Diet of bone worms and putrified rat!
Strike off his name from the life-worthy list!

Palestrina

Palestrina!—that looks down
upon its valley and out and
away to other heights through
ancient eyes that gleamed with
civilized light a thousand years
before the birth of Christ!

WHITE-SOLED UPON A CLOUD

In Palestrina we two walked white-soled upon a cloud
That rose and covered us. You said, "It clings!—softly!"
                                                "Like a shroud,"
I quipped. You tossed a frown at *that* idea. I laughed. We both
   laughed—
And romped and rolled through the misty mantle. You said,
   "We're daft!"
"But never dead!" *I* said. "And if we *were*!—we'd have no need
Of grave-garb: cloud or linen or *any* covering decreed
By church or state!"

                    And I say now: In *that* Italian altitude
We'd be covered by understanding, and we'd not be named nude
Though we foolish-died as shiny-bare as two old milking stools
In Palestrina—up and above the eyes of "worldly" fools!

How Thin!

Today again we climbed to Palestrina—and bought
Copper jugs and bowls, and amphorae, and bas-reliefs—
And laces from a woman who showed cheerful griefs
In willing, damaged fingers and in eyes that had caught
Smile-tragic loss of all her sons—all six—hers a life
Of endless, crippling toil!—

But oh! I thought: If *I* could wield
the knife
That would slash from human race the wanton-stupid sin
Of needless want that drives such lowly-darling "peasant" sisters
To work their bowed and wrinkled body parts to blisters
For a lousy bite of bread and—

Then I stopped. Christ! How thin!
"If *I* could!" I! Nuts! I!—so goddamned busy cherishing *my* skin!

AGAIN TO PALESTRINA

Again, *again* we rose to Palestrina, and now found (how, *how*
Did we forget?) that here the *genius* "Palestrina" learned to
  live and grow!
"Palestrina"!—you, the *man,* the *once* man!—*you,* the long-*gone*
man!—
You, the *dead* man!—*you,* the past-living prince of musical crea-
  tion,
Gone-alive now, but then, then, in going, borne to grave-rest
On time-growing liturgy, sweet-snatched from *your* work, notes
  that ran
Before you, with you, after you, to mark your hand on *nation*
That, with *your* soul-reach, in beauty, soared in classic *sweep* to
  that creative crest!

Observation in a Roman Saloon

A girl comes into a stylish bar,
Sits in a room where "gentlemen" are.
Far she is, far from a conscious fear,
From dread of contempt, its knowing sneer:

(She has a business, she sells her love.
She feels no more than the need to prove
She's worth the price of an hour of bed,
Of her own sad need: a bit of bread.)

But cold contempt and heartless using
Are hers, and God knows what abusing!

And I *don't* believe she likes it all,
Is dead to the fears she had when small.
The childish dread of a stranger's hands,
Obscenity's breath, and brutal demands.

So let her come into the stylish bar
And sit in the room where "gentlemen" are,
And let the "gentlemen" pay and use her.
But may God punish the ones that abuse her!

A Dinner in Pisa

Now see:
I spent a dinner, in Pisa, with certain friends.
We ate and talked. . . . I have heard asked: "What are the ends
Of social itch?" Ha! *You* want to meet people with *names?*
You want to be seen as one of a lean-assed *lot* of names?
It would oblige *you* to read in a Pisa paper
That you, *you* dined and drank and cut a caper?

Great balls! . . . We ate dinner! And how we drank and spoke!
And I tell *you!—I* was a laugh *hit* when I told my joke!
And those great people there? *"Peasants!" All!—loving* thereness!
And not one preoccupied with self-conscious awareness!
Except *me!*

Confession in Palermo

I met a girl tonight.
Me, I'm not as young as numbered springs.
But this girl, this child
Was lovely—and I thought of things
Beyond me. Mind you,
Not for a moment—or a *stingy* moment—
Did the male in me
Assert itself. Good grief! *I* should foment
In this ripe hulk
Such amorous ambition? No, really no,
I did not. But—oh,
Is there man of sere-ish, unsmall year
Who never sheds
(Not I, not I!) a ghostly, bone-dry tear?

'TIS PITY WE'RE ASHORE

The seamen have "struck," and here in Rome
We make believe that we're snug at home.
But we're really not snug, and home is so far
We're farther by far than the seamen are
From home and the feel and the smell of home,
Trapped in this palace in *Cesare's* Rome!

For they've "struck" and we're stuck in this splendid city
That's losing its splendor . . . and more's the pity!

Rome—1959

"THERE'S NO PLACE—!"

Home is the one place that oh! we know so surely
Is *surely* home when we're away-*away* from home!
Why home should never, never quite so purely
Be *all* of home but from another land is some
Problem to be solved by better brains than brains
That find nepenthe in dull doggerel droppings!—brains
That—body-freed!—should find a perch of reasoning
On poles!—unpeopled poles!—and squat for lifetimes,
In ponder style, to isolate and *null* the seasoning
Pinched by poet to *sharpen* taste of home in rhymes,
In rhymes, in rhymes!—that stab homesickness a *thousand* times!

LAMENT OF TOURIST

The world is made up of *us*, dear friend,
Yes, of you and me.
I live my life where I live, and you yours
Here in Italy.

But what, in the name of intelligence,
I cannot see
Is why you, dear friend, here in Italy,
Can't live like me!

LIMERICKS

Line Written in Anticipation of the Recitation of Certain Bawdy Jingles

The cloth of the limerick's coat
Is cut from the groin of a goat.
So throttle your noses,
And don't expect roses,
You won't hear a word you can quote

Concerning Gertie Stein and "Alice, the Toklas"

Said Gertrude to Alice, "Peugh! Grammar!
Please strike me again with that hammer."
When Alice demurred,
Gertie howled, "You're absurd!
How else can I write with a stammer?"

"I don't want to snork," said Phil Double-you
Or to niggle or nozzle or nubble you.
"But why is a Frenchman
Called 'French?'—while a henchman
Called 'Hench' would be something to trouble you?"

Paris—1955

"It is true," José sighed, in Peru
Even pigs have the fragrance of rue
      Mosquitoes make honey,
      You live without money
And people find pearls in their Stew!"
Geneva—June 21, 1955

Our Schnooks is a logical lass,
She thinks about Moscow at Mass,
      She dearly hates commies,
      But thinks Atom bombies
Should blow up McCarthy, that ass!
Geneva—June 21, 1955

A couple got married in court,
On a dog license made out to "Sport,"
      The judge called their room
      And exclaimed to the groom,
"If you ain't done it, don't, it ain't for't."

Thoughts on St. Patrick's Day

An Irish colleen named O'Venus
Took hold of a gentleman's penis.
      Said she, "Let's undress,
      Then when I confess
I can say there was nothing between us."

A wood carver came to Doc Little
Complaining of gunk in his spittle,
    "A cinch!" cried the Doc
    "Just take off a sock
And suck your big toe while you whittle!"

Limerick Lines written in the belief that the true medical genius always
prescribes the simple remedy.

Young Michael, the son of wee Annie
Has a trick with a gun that's uncanny,
    With aim that is dead
    He shoots straight ahead
And hits himself smack in the fanny.

Said Mills, "I take pills for my ills;
For I'm cursed with a gripe of the gills,
    Just one shot of Scotch
    And the notch of my crotch
Is invaded by porcupine quills."

The lady was chic as a button.
"We live over East; you know; Sutton?"
    She spoke of Tebaldi,
    Of Proust and Vivaldi—
Then greased up her chin—wolfing mutton!

My aunt, with a splendid conviction,
Chewed Webster to sharpen her diction.
      Her molars fell out,
      To prove, without doubt,
That tooth is *not* stronger than friction.

Said John, "I sell business machines.
I sell them by any old means
      I sold one to Venus
      By means of my penis—
Hush, sweetie, you know I hate scenes!"

There once was a lovely named Rita,
Who moved with the grace of a cheetah.
      Said she, "It's not hard,
      I just bathe in lard
And rub motor oil on my seata."

"Look, sweetie," said Rita to Rick,
"It's really a little bit thick.
      If *you* keep on bitchin'
      When I'm in my kitchen,
I'll wallop your bum with a stick!"

Said Ricky to Rita, "Look, flounder,
Two women have walloped my schmounder.
      The one doesn't smell
      Cause I gave her nose hell;
The other smells awful. I drowned 'er."

"I'm kind!" snarled the captain. "By crickey!—
My NCOs call me 'Big Ricky!'
    I baby my privates
    With drill sharp at five, it's
The bastards' own fault if I'm sticky!"

Said da Vinci, (just finished with "Lisa")
"I think I'll hop over to Pisa.
    I hear there's a steeple
    Where grin-sickened people
Can climb, lean and puke without visa."

We Had A Lack
Of Cadillac
Alack, Alack
No More!

Our new car is quite the fromage,
A chrome, paint and crystal mirage.
I can drive up the street
For at least ninety feet
And its end hasn't left the garage.

"I admit it!" howled drenched Miss de Peughs,
"My passion is sharp as new screws!
But barfly or Duke,
A man is a schnook,
When he tries out for sex in canoes!"

Be quiet!" cried Pop Hermie Schmierkase.
"I state, as an obvious clear case:
That a man isn't old
Till his bottom is cold
And he sneers at the goods from a beer case!"

As Sandy taught scales to a Turk
He opened his pants with a smirk.
"My landy!" said Sandy,
"I'll admit it's a dandy,
But you *must* do your *own* finger work."

Should We Not Face Ourselves?

By the laws of defense, if none other,
There are children that mothers should smother.
　　　When I was an urchin
　　　I *would* fart in church'n
Throw dry pony turds at my brother.

Were I just a common repeater,
I'd repeat myself often in meter.
　　　If a man loves his wife,
　　　She's more than his life,
So he's not very likely to beat her.

A Riddle
*Guess Who, or What**

The owl's lovely shipmate: sweet riddle!
Instrumentalist: hi diddle, diddle!
　　　As soft as wee rabbits
　　　With excellent habits,
She loves someone much, me a liddle.

---
*Our cat FIDDLE.

I'd like for to find me the gumption
To land bruising boots on the rumption
     Of fools, who, assumin'
     That *my* cat ain't human
Deny her a soul! Such presumption!

You ask for my autograph. (Sigh!)
But "a few lines of handwriting." Why?
     Are you *that* "Penman" Ashley
     Who raises checks rashly?
If so, keep them low, please. Bye-bye!

And now from the ring that is Kessel,
"If some of you girls like to wrestle
     Just loosen your tights
     And we'll turn out the lights;
I know several holds that are special."

Some time ago the name "Otto de Pung" came
to the author. He decided that only a
murderously filthy fellow could have such a
nasty name.
Then, behold ('twas the month of December)
"Awful Otto" tied himself to the Christmas
season and laid hold of the author's pen.

The result: " 'Tis Christmas," Sighed Otto de Pung,
     'Tis time for the greens to be hung."

After that he couldn't stop Otto!

CK

" 'Tis Christmas," sighed Otto de Pung,
" 'Tis time for the Greens to be hung."
      And soon, from a halter,
      The Greens, Bess and Walter,
Were dangling and going, "Glung, glung!"

"I'm gentle," sighed Otto de Pung,
"I'm especially kind to the young.
      I never throw babies
      To dogs that have rabies,
The thought of it leaves me unstrung!"

Cute Otto de Pung, the old stink!—
Spread salt on the ice-skating rink.
      As skaters went down
      Otto smirked, "I'm a clown!
Let's hope the whole lot of them sink!"

Said Otto de Pung, " 'Nasty' Ned?
Last Monday I cut the man dead!
      From instep to guzzle
      I've minced him! The puzzle
Is just what to do with his head!"

Young Otto de Pung, (worthy scion)
Helped Grandpa de Pung put his tie on.
    As Grandfather strangled,
    Good Otto, heart mangled,
Used Grandpa's fat wallet to cry on.

"Dear neighbors," cried Otto, "don't beller!
I keep all my snakes in the cellar!"
    But neighbors gulped mirth
    When a cobra gave birth
To a limbless girl-child, spitting yeller.

Good Otto de Pung woke in bed
With a young lady's torso—quite dead!
    "Oh, bother!" he cried,
    "I just can't abide
A woman who loses her head!"

Said Otto de Pung—the old sinner!—
"I think I'll have young Brown for dinner."
    So Brown, stewed with spices,
    Was served in thin slices.
"Delicious!" cried Otto. "A winner!"

Young Otto de Pung (he was drunk)
Had an intimate pass with a skunk.
     His triplets, much later,
     Laid claim on their pater. . . .
He chased them. . . . Said Otto, "They stunk!"

"Give tongue!" cried de Pung. "Never quaver!
The Bible *commands*: 'Love thy neighbor!'
     My neighbor, named 'May,'
     I love!—*twice* a *day!*
She's married to Benedict Faber."

De Pung, the Hero

The train came on fast—chung! Chung—Chung!
Bunched low in the ditch was de Pung.
     The train struck his log
     And plowed deep in the bog.
One person was saved—young de Pung!

Good Otto de Pung's Uncle Breaut
Had a quite most remarkable flute,
     He'd blow with a will
     And a cute poisoned pill
Would be lodged in the green-grocer's fruit.

"Sopranos," sighed Otto de Pung,
"Have tongues like a scooping of dung.
    But roasted till brown
    One *can* get them down.
And *think* of the *singing* un*sung!*"

Said Otto de Pung, "Just between us,
I'm a wonderful man with my penis.
    When I was an urchin
    I'd pull off in church'n
Then lay every female but Venus!"

Good Otto de Pung flew to France,
Where he saw ladies dance without pants,
    Back home in Schmooguire,
    He stripped his fem choir. . . .
His choir's all gone now! Romance!

Sweet Otto de Pung met his preacher—
And the preacher's wife, Flo, Bible teacher.
    The preacher's glad-wild
    With de Pung's second child.
But de Pung doesn't brag. It's his feature!

Good Otto de Pung met a Saint:
A Virgin she was, without taint.
    They walked down the track
    Till they came to a shack. . . .
De Pung's fine. The virgin? She ain't!

Methinks Good Otto Braggeth

"I'm de Pung—(of the ancient de Pungs).
Our prime festive dish is skunk lungs.
    Our *peasants* eat pheasants,
    Skunk lungs need the presence
Of keen, nobly-bred de Pung tongues."

De Pung joined the Salvation Army.
Said he, "Well, it can't do no harmy"
    I stand on a bench
    And swear in bad French,
And dopes toss me money. *Who's* barmy?"

Good Otto de Pung, (the old silly!)
Sharp severed the throat of wee Willy.
    When Willy's fond kin
    Called the action a sin,
Otto chortlingly sighed, "Willy Nilly!"

Young Otto de Pung—'twas a tussle!—
Stuffed rats in his grandmother's bustle.
"You darling!" cried Granny,
"They do gnaw my fanny!
But they make such an elegant rustle!"

As Otto was strolling Westminster,
He took the blue eyes of a spinster.
"Of course," he'll confide,
"The poor old thing died.
A shame. I had nothing aginst 'er."

A Closing Note

To be tops in one's field?—to be sung
As outstanding man, men among?—
This *right* peak is valid!
So let's not be pallid:
Our finest foul *crud* is *de Pung!*

Lines Written for Good and Dear Old Fell, M.D.

Said "Fell" of the medical section,
"Hypochondria's worse than infection.
That pain in your heart, ma'am,
Is only a phart, ma'am,
With very poor sense of direction!"

Doc Fell—(Ah, such cases were bliss!)
Had a lass with a bad kidney hiss.
        Said he, "You should oughter
        Drink plenty of water
And stand on your head when you s-s-s-s-s."

Said "Fell" in a mood of reflection,
"I'm open, of course, to correction.
        But wouldn't it seem
        That Futility's dream
Was a eunuch's posthumous erection?"

An M.D. named Fell, pondered—said:
"I treat certain patients in bed.
        I find, my technique,
        When we lie cheek to cheek
Is just *right!—if* the lady's not dead."

Growled good Dr. Fell, "It's obscene!
Ovarian cysts turn me green!
        You slice in, all jolly—
        Go 'spin!'—then, by golly!
Out pops a sweet-tooth tangerine!"

Said Fell (a remarkable surgeon),
"I've tried finding caviar in sturgeon.
  The fishes I've cut
  Would distend a whale's gut,
But the sturgeon I've cut are all virgin!"

Doc Fell was a whiz with his knife
"Snip-snip" and he'd rescue a life.
  He had on the table
  A lady named Mable. . . .
She died. . . . She was Dr. Fell's wife!

An M.D. named Fell probed a lung
(His patient was named O. de Pung),
  When Fell struck a pebble,
  De Pung howled in treble—
(the bell for *Fell's* funeral has rung).

STRANGER AT THE GATE

Like a bag of rags he leaned on a vacant anthill, well inside
my gate.
I slowed my stroll, paused, peered. He made no move to leave,
no stirring move to rise;
Made no slightest move—except to twitch his garbled nose, spit
and turn his eyes.
"Spare the worn word, good m'lord," he said. "Bethink. Swallow
the dreary cliche, mate;

"You know: 'Private property! Be gone! Be off, fellow! Scram!'
—or—'Can I help you?' . . .
You look the book-rule 'decent type' that might say, 'Can I help
you?' Eh, m'lord?"
He was a mangy one, battered, filthy, spent, his sick lips blue-
bruised and scored
By bleeding cracks, his scruffy neck death-wasted. And he wore
but *one shoe.*

His palsied hands had scabby knuckle wounds, gnarled fingers,
black nails broken to the raw.
One ear was fat, bloated to the dead-flesh likeness of a new-
sprung puffball.
Something—a brutal blow?—had spread his nose obscenely. Some-
thing—a drunken fall?—
Had torn his cheek, warped his chin, smashed the front teeth,
four of them, out of his lower jaw.

His clothes were old-time gypsy discards—crusty-foul—though
his jacket held a tweedy
Hint of Scottish looming. A rope held up the bags he used for
pants. No words
Could name the greasy, matted tangle on his head. Hair? A per-
fect home for birds!
He stank of alcoholic vomit. I sickened, groped, seized upon the
one shoe oddity.

"It's been a long night," I said. "It's nearly noon. You'll be late
for the Duchess.

"And I'm not the 'decent type' at all. But no shoes are better than one—
For *walking*. If you catch my point." "S'truth, m'lord. And two shoes are better than none. . . .
"And you, sire: without feet—" he drew a jackknife, opened it— "you'd go with crutches.

"I'd say you wear nines or tens. Yes? Why, so do I! My lucky day, uh? Uh, m'lord?"
He tapped the knife blade on his knee—twisted a broken lip— looked at me. . . .
He sour-laughed. "Some people go all pale and queasy at a knife. They pee."
I stood there—*had* to smile. "Well, all right," he said, "*don't* pee. But don't pretend you're bored!"

"Not bored," I said, "concerned. Concerned about *you*. Your date with the Duchess, you know.
Perfect morning for a walk." . . . The poor lips thinned. He said, "It's my habit
To go deaf to brutal mouthings that infer my kin to 'dog' or 'pig'—or '*rabbit!*' "
He bit the word. "Surprise, uh? No stinking bum could possibly know 'Alice'? No!"

He paused long . . . scratched, grinned. "So sorry. Well, now! This 'walking': See!—I walked from a grave
In Minnesota! I started yesterday—and yesterday and yesterday is the time that stopped! Eh?
Ha! Ho, ho! *Dead* time? *I* know it! Sire, it has merit! It's such a cinch to *save!*"

He laughed again, coughed harshly, spat, wiped blood from his lips with a wounded fist.

"Well, well! That's settled. It's plain you're up with me. Just relativity. So, now, sire,
About the 'walking': Your nourished fingers: press them to 'this sorry scheme of things entire,'
Squeeze till it squeals 'Here's justice! Mark! *Walking should be paid for!*' Ha! And truth be pissed!

"And if it shouldn't? It's work, ain't it? It surely *do* be! And I, as says so, *knows!*
And further word! Your bible! Plain as paint! '*The laborer is worthy of his hire!*'
But cripes, m'lord, what's this? My very arse is rosy at my crude appeal! Good sire,
I'll level with you. *All this is just to touch you where the lovely hand-out grows!*

"Not that I'm planted here in limpid anguish, appealing for a *bone.*
I've had my fill of bones. In fact, my skin's so Christly full of them, they jut.
So not a bone, sire—not a rancid doughnut, moldy hash. I'm *not* a mut.
I know, because I know, by God, I—still can laugh and cry—and use a phone!"

What is it in us that leads us, carelessly, against our kindness, to be cruel?
I said, "I've read of dogs that laugh, and mother bears that cry. And on tee-vee
I watched a monkey make a phone call. And there's a mule, I think in Missouri—"
I stopped. He was quite slumped—head, shoulders—quite; shriveled, a dwarfed, inhuman fool.

I could not dissolve, so I said, "Fifty cents—what would you do with—? no! Ten times fifty!"

That stirred him. "Why, noble man! Why, sire, you *fraud!* Good
well you know I'd buy a crock
Of ghinny red! The damndest-God-damned-biggest-God-damned
crock they'd have in stock!
Or 'Sneaky Pete'! Five dollars worth? Ha! I'd have the added
jolt of being thrifty!"

"Yeah, man!" I said. "And when you'd killed the crock?" His eyes
refused, held to my belt buckle.
"You son-of-a-bitch!" he whispered. There never was a placid
answer to that one.
So I stood there, empty of any word, knowing that, oh, no!—this
was *not* fun—
As he drooped, *all* body drooped, broken, mouth closing emptily
on his knuckle.

I could hear him, just. "No," he said. "The dream, the vision.
Booze?—pre-swallowed vomit? No."
(Without the teeth he had to gum the knuckle.) "Not ever. . . .
No. Not *any* day."
I was beside him now, squatting. He stirred, drew back. "Okay.
You're close enough, Padre."
I said, "What is your dream?" He made a sound. Contempt for
me? Despair? I didn't know. . . .

Finally he said, "Right. Right-O. . . . It's not of booze, no part
of booze. Or God's a liar and a thief!
Not stinking oblivion, my vision! And oh, Christ, not the puking
in agony!—
Of sickness beyond the comprehension of *hell! Not! Please!"*—
I *felt* his sickness—in *me.*
I said, "Tell me. You *can,* friend. What is your vision?" He col-
lapsed into soundless grief.

I held him. He no longer drew away. He wept *on* me, with me.
The wish to prove

Anything at all was not in me now. I felt guilty, stupidly presumptuous!
To unman a pride that covered grief beyond the *ever* knowing
of the most of us!—
So, as he wept, and *I* wept, I thought: this is the desolation of
all lost love. . . .

Exhaustion stilled him. When he straightened, all grace had left
him, I thought; all power
To pretend, to force the quip, the covering phrase and accent;
almost all life. His belly
Quivered. He swayed. (*Now* I wondered when he'd last had
food!—*now!* My *own* guts made like jelly.)
But still he was his man; *pretending* he had just, oh, reached to
pick a clover flower!

He picked it, steadied, drew up, turned. . . . Then, for the first
time, I saw his eyes. They fastened
On mine, blood-sick, pewter-dull—but steady, purpose-level—as
though now, and *just* now
He had chosen to *let* me see them—and see *him.* If that *was* his
purpose I didn't know—
But I did see him, strangely, as not before! And mine were the
eyes that fell, chastened.

His gaze was not a challenge, not a rebuke, it went with the
the nature of his voice
When he spoke, low, dully. "I've finished with nonsense, friend,"
he said. "You've been patient, bless you.
My dream, my vision is quite simple; quite *insane,* as 'simple'
means, or used to.
My vision is the psychopathic dreaming of a rot-brained drunk
who has the choice

"Of dream stuff or reality! But no!—what drool—reality in al-
cohol?

107

Nuts! But cripes, m'lord!—(No! No more of that 'm'lord' stuff, friend!

Dis-ball me else!) Look, man, look! This is the point!—the nit-wit silly end!

But please don't snort! Think just that it's the nature of a drunk to dream so tall!

"Friend!—*my vision is the hefting in my hand of money!* Oh!—so much, much money!

Sometimes in my *drunkest* dreams I touch it! You know! A roll, a finger-bulging wad!

Not 'ones'! No! In my hand the swollen feel of *hundreds!* So that I—oh, God, *God!*—

So that I—so that my heart—!" (He broke.) "All right! Go ahead, snort! God knows it's funny!—"

"Wait, now, wait," I said. "Just tell me. The dream, the vision: I know you now, a bit;

There must be more than just a miser itch to—well—it's sort of out of sense."

But he was sitting there—one hand gripping the other. I woke from my pretense.

"When you'd have this visionary money—*If* you had it, what would you do with it?"

Those crippled hands tore at each other. He rocked. That seeming scarecrow, that broken man

Tore *me* with his passion of heartbreak. "I'd go back!" he croaked. "I'd go back to that grave!

And I'd speak to it and touch it! And I'd spill my tears on it and beg her to save

Me! And I'd tell her what she wants to hear! What *she,* down under there, can, *can*

"Hear, wants, wants, *someplace* wants to hear! That I'll do and be what she wants of me!—

108

Wants me to be! That I can! *be!* that I *can!*—" He collapsed like
a dropped cup. *All* done.
Then—"By God!" I thought. "How false *am* I? Playing Samaritan!
Yes! Having fun!—
Adventure!" And thought, "How *thick* am I? The time it takes
for decision to come clear to me!"

And thought of times past when cowardice had taken me, *fear*
that I'd be branded
"Easy mark" or "sucker" by "level heads" and "realists" for giving
in impulsive
Gesture! "Ha!" they'd say. "They'll laugh at you, old boy! You're
a mugg!" Thought of those times I've
Muttered, "Sorry," and scuttered on—possibly leaving desperation
empty handed.

Well! My father held that boys—in fact, anybody—should always
carry
"Panic" money. A dollar. Now I carry hundreds, deeply tucked
away someplace.
He felt, bless him, that sometime, somewhere—who knew?—there
might be possible ungrace
If one were "caught without funds." What if one *had* to take a
cab—(or go to Rome, or marry)?

My father had the wisdom of a tree: green leaves, countless,
always someplace handy.
That had a lot to do with what I felt when my friend rose and
stumped away. My weight,
Under my bare feet, irked me rather pleasantly as he booted
past the gate.
He turned, once, gestured to my wave, said "God bless!" . . . I
thought, "Dear me, *I* need a brandy!"

109

OH, BLESSED COMPANY!
A COCKTAIL PARTY!

There is a certain type of headache, a certain brow sweat,
A certain queasy anguish of the belly that seem to
Overtake me—in what was a sweet-aired, restful room—
While hosting for the entertainment of company most any:
Dear people, kindly minds, friends, chaps and ladies I've met
Lately, ago, last night; good souls all—*most* all—(I do *not* dislike
People!)—learned comrades, sweet neighbors, worthy fellow
   hacks—
But a mass, a group of humanoids; a mob, a bunch, or even
Six faces!—Anyway—oh, *always!—they've* been invited.

So papers, socks, the cat's pan, scurfy slippers, hung-stale towels—
(Not soiled, just hung-stale)—shorts, worn cushions, my shower
Derby, (people ask why!) my flute, and "Fanny Hill," thumbed,
Well thumbed and open on the reading couch, (people pry!)
The cat's "foul" play toys: (she thinks they're splendid, so do I!)
Felt balls, a "billious" fish, six "mangy," mouselike mice,
Plastic balls, a "leprous" leopard, a "filthy" bean-fat frog—

All such couthless things I've stashed in groaning places:
Shelves, drawers, closets, two blushing tuck-ins underneath

The dog-eared sofas. (The Rodin double-nude *stays* out!)

They arrive: those snap-eyed, ever-red-faced first arrivers.
"Well!" says she. "We *thought*—!"—and censures *me* with smiling
teeth.
(*I'm* to blame! I told folks nine-ish, it's now well after ten!)

Four more arrive. (Ah, she forgives me!) ... They all arrive!
(They *are* nice people. A warming, laughing chatter fills the
room.
I chatter. I feel *good!*) Drinks: gin, scotch and rye and bourbon
Drinks, and beer—and vodka drinks because they're smart as
New-laid Paris hats—are ordered, poured and swallowed.

And then we sit. And talk. And drink and smoke—and drink. . . .

Sheila Tackyew, languid-leaning over "Boo" the lady lure,
Asks for "irish panther pee." I make a laugh sound as "Boo"
whinnies.
(I feel the brushing touch of queasiness.) "So sorry, love,
"No irish. Have a scotch and lysol." (Me, I'm funny too.)

Madam Red "A"—panther-tawny, lushly busty-hippystacked—
Ice-eyes Sheila, pouts a wordless message: "Dear!—you should
be dead!—
And 'Boo' in bed—and not alone!" (Her two-ton husband hind-
ers.)
Can he have heard that lyric bit: "Oh, pipe the lay of Little
Neck, L.I.!"?
They live in Little Neck. I golf there. (The room is getting
stuffy.)

Refills, refills, and fills beyond "re" disappear.
(My head aches.) Some several happy friends become unboned,
Ooze floorward liver-legged, squat cosily—sans ash trays, coasters,
Wits and dribble bibs. (I munch a soda mint. I yawn. It's two!)

Time goes. . . . Good Christian White, my dear old buddy-chum
   (I met him
In a pub two nights ago) is rumbling mouth sounds to a group.
I catch a word. Well, well!—it's "jigaboo"!—another—and I *think*—
Yes, there it is again! It's "jew"! (My "buddy-chum" is in
The "wrecking game," he told me.) Ah, good Ouimus speaks!
   Stout fellow!

(Ouimus Albee-Bigger: Oxford throated, teaches Abstract His-
   tory
At Vassar.) "Quate, quate!" he quates. "But easy on! we mahst be
"Tolerant!" (Oh, dandy! Let's "tolerate" the "lesser breeds"! Eh,
   what?)
"Tola-unt?"—(Good Christian has a south-pole southern ac-
   cent.)—
"Wha, summa ma baist fraind are—! Ah'm broadmahnded!"
   (Shall we vomit?)
"Who, *me?*—a *southna'?* Well, fra ma spleen! Ah'm Yankee! Boan
   an' raised in
Boaston, Mass! Lived in Jojuh fo' a spell is oall!—a yeeah—

Damn neeah." Did I *invite* this creep? (It's three. My middle
burns!)

Bicarb!—that should help! I slither-sidle-ease to exit—*but!*—
My closed-door bedroom!—my me-sagged, *private bed!*—they're
occupied!
Priapismic "Boo", and Madam Red "A"—! Gee-zuz! (No!—I *won't*
puke!)
His wife twelve feet away!—her anthropoidal husband just *out*
there!

(Who minds hot murder? Hardly they! *I* don't pay rent to house
it!
And who's embarrassed? Neither "Boo" nor Madam "A"!) Sweet
trollop:
"I really was *so* sick!" . . . "She tossed her beans!" . . . "And Booey
held my head!" . . .
"Yeah, head! I'm like her brother! You know, Fam'ly!" *Gee*-zuz!
I *smile.*
"*Well,* then, that's not so bad—just *incest!* Perhaps I should
apologize!
But zip your fly!" . . . I must seem *quite* disturbed. Tight-smiling,
dart-eyed,
They back-step out like *things* before a lifted sharp-nailed stick.

The soda helps a mite—for just a mite. But in the hallway
Myna Hardlott, tipsy-weepy, talons me to cry on—as I burp.
Nothing special-griefy in her life. It's just that all and more
And everything is "hurty-hard" to bear! (I'm such a damn good
Shoulder patter! She really wets my chest! I inch to break:

I have a toothache in the back of both my knees.) And then
She says:—(she's really nice, you know; straight, clean and kind,
And sober-clever)—She says: "Life seems to be just one long run
In a stocking!" ("By george," I think, "that's good! I'll swipe it!"
    And so
I *have* to break!—to jot it down. I lose these things so quickly.)

Time goes. . . . Goes? It giggles, shrieks and bellows through the
    night—
At snail's pace. (Yet it's *four!*) I have a moment, frayed: What if
    I howl
Alarmingly?—collapse a bit, froth, vibrate, scare the water
Out of all or sundry, scare them into sober thoughts of homing?
But howling to collapse is bad for headaches. And anyway!—

I spot four trusties, heads close, gabbing in a corner island.
I swim to them through seas of ruptured tonsils, smoking tongues!
Bellies burst to right and left and bowelish laughter nearly
swamps me!
My elbow sweeps! . . . I *make it!* They welcome me!—without
    a shriek
Or sob or back massage! I sit. What bliss!—they're talking
    theatre!—
Soberly! (My knee teeth lose their ache.) Oh, happy hour!

I talk! (Our heads are all together, damning out the rising

Tide of bedlam—we think!) I've touched upon my second act:
"The man," I say, "*seems* crazy but he's not; that is, he's not
Supposed to be; I mean, I have the feeling often that he is!
Don't get me wrong," I say. "I'm writing 'Hamlet,' sure, but what
I mean,
The thing's not '*Hamlet*'! Oh, maybe 'Hamletish," as Pirandello
Might have—well, you know, the hung-up ending?—leave'm
guessing?—
'Nuts he is or nuts he's not?—who knows?' But look: he loves his
mother
So damn much he hates her guts—but humorously, you know?
Well, in the second act—" . . . Great Poxy Peter! The dam is
breached!

"You five!" shrills Eve. "You're spoiling all the party, talking
shop!"
"The evangels!" Adam roars. "Discussing sin! Just let *us* in!
We're experts!" Damn that pair! They *do* live in it: sin! And
never
Miss a chance to shout the fact! (A frightened halfwit's ego
prop!)

"Cal, dahling," flutes "Aunt Mame," (she loved the play) "you've
got to
Settle something! Who painted Frank Hall's 'Laughing Boy'? Or
did he?"
"*I* said he *did!*" big Tina squeals. "But not Frank Hall at all!"
Poor Cal. He pales and panics, having faced ten thousand foolish
Painty-questions from the great thumb-fingered hordes of bud-
ding "Hals' "—

But none like this. Off he goes like "Hyde"—a twitching, giggling
   ruin.

I turn. Jim Oast is crouched upon the floor behind his chair!
(He prints fine prints on fabrics.) Bending hawklike, poised to
   strike
His eyes out, "home-soul" Bidda Pennymore raspy-coos to him
About his "remlets." He *must* have "remlets"! Yards and yards
Of "remlets"! She's "desprit"! She's doing over living room and
   all!
Of course, she'll pay!—not much but—"Here! Where *are* you go-
   ing?"
(I never thought a man could creep so fast!) . . . And Ted and
   Deirdre?

Lost!—lost, too, these trusties! "Fatso" Funiman—(he's TV's gift
To laughter—but not lately) enfolds them with his forty-five
Pound arms! He has a *big* idea! "Enormouse! Wow! A *musical!*
Now, wait! A *funny* show, a *really* funny show! The 'book'?
The *only* one! You'll *really* flip!" It's "Pullman Named Retire.")

"Look, Deirdre!—" (Deirdre *agents* "Pullman." She blinks, she
   shudders, sways.)
"Look, Ted!—" (Ted *lawyers* "Pullman." His cheek goes jumping
   tickishly.)
"That rape scene!" ("Fatso" has a sprayed-saliva sell.) "A boffo!
I'll use my dead-pan act! Man, man! Backed up with nice rape
   music?—"

119

She does *not* hit him—Deirdre; her elbow merely swings in reel-
ing.
And Teddy's foot, sharp-shock-convulsed, leaps up and out quite
unbeknownst
To Ted. He does *not* kick great "Fatso" in the ass. But no!

These trusties, both are two-drink people, strictly, and having
had
Their two they won't drink more;—that is—ah, me!—they will
and *do!*

So I'm alone, alone again—in bedlam—and slipping rapidly
Into a state of coma; waking-aching, walking-talking coma.

A lady, weaving, peers into my shirt front and says I look so
happy.
"It *is* a lovely party, you dear rascal!"—and she's so glad,
So glad, so glad, so glad, so glad—(now, wait, ol'-boy-ol'-rascal!
She gave with that glady-glad an hour ago!—or was it two?
Take hold, wake up, get hosty! They're *all* here for-because you
asked them!
You need a little drink, ol' rasc, a little clearing cloud-sweep!) . . .

"Ah, thanks, dear! I did say 'little' but—oh, well, here's bottoms
up!"
"*No*, dear, *no*, I didn't mean it lit'rally!" . . . "Well, then, if you
must!"
(Great Venus!) "Oh, *no*, pet, not *offended! I* brought the whole
thing up!

That is, I don't mean 'thing'! I mean, not *yours!*— *bottom,* that is!
I mean—!" (Ye gods! The saving grace of drunken ladies' pants!)

At any rate, it seems I'm rising out of alcoholic coma.
By lift of *alcohol?* Oh, well—I see and hear and smell
And feel again! Or is that good?—to see and hear and smell—
And feel like hell! Oh, well! "Nothing lasts forever, brother!"
And time *is* passing, surely. *Surely!* I'll just be philosophic.
Of course time passes! . . . And *Sheila* passes!—yeah, man!—*semi-
out!*
Perhaps the scotch and lysol—? No such luck. . . . Ooops!—she
up-chucks!
Now, *why*—? Oh, well! She *almost* hit the fireplace, dear harpy!

Ah, laughter! Good clean fun! "It's likker makes a party go!"

("Go? Good God, why *don't* they?—*go,* I mean! It's twenty after
five!)

And then they do! They *go!* They *leave, go, all* of them!—almost
Abruptly!—with many a cunning doorward urge by merry-host—

And I'm *alone!* . . . I lean. Ah, me, ah, me!—alone—with the stink
of them,
The mess of them, the burned-black craters-in-the-rug of them!—

The people (some I love!) who ringed my Steinway! And *I*
  asked them!
Am *I* the damnedest bottle-headed fool in missile distance!

I dry-weep. I don't feel *good*. Good? Great holy smoke!—I'm
  sick!

And then begins that *mortal* head pain, that wringing brow
  sweat,
That wet-green, curling nausea that calls for warm salt-water's
Horrid mercy, icy cloths, pills, capsules, swallowed balm
And bed, bed, bed!—with the pop-skull hope that worthy Beulah,
Soft-walking, kindly Beulah will soft-walk in like Beulah—
(But late, late, late, dear Beulah!)—and repair the devastation
Without disturbing master till he's slept, slept, slept, (please,
  Beulah!)
And healed sufficiently to plan another cozy little necessary
Get-together—get-together—get-to—Oh, dear! God help me!

MY WORLD, MY WIFE

Hurt That Never Cries

She stood awkwardly beneath an awkward tree.
She was an awkward child of twenty-three.
He moved gracefully across the field and toward the wood—
And found the awkward tree—and her, there, where she stood—
And found no awkwardness in tree, or child— but eyes
That were beauty—beneath a *kindly* tree—great eyes
That spoke compassion, truth—and hurt that never cries.

Oh, damn the world, that locks us in a bond
That says to us: Peace, peace, there's something more beyond.
And yet—why should we damn the world that's of our making?
We said: "We'll take this world, and all, forsaking
What a dream world promised. Well, then, let us *take*
This world. And forsake that other world as simply a mistake.

The Weight of Waiting

Sometimes the weight of waiting
becomes more heavy than
the weight of one who waits.

Waiting has a built-in hopelessness
that grows out of all proportion
to the time of waiting.

Waiting moments have no kinship
with reasonable judgment
with evidence of clock time!

Waiting "moments," given to the true clock,
would stretch man's hour to days,
and days to agonies of endless time.

Cynic's Confusion

It's night. I can't find it in my fingers to write
Seriously of "things that go bump in the night"!
But the world is full of "children" who wake in fright,
Cold-sweaty fright at "things that go bump in the night."
Yet *I* take cynical, superior delight
In my mockery of the fear that wails for light
To chase the "thing" that's near! . . . Oh, but I'm right, eh?—
    right?—
There *is* no dreadful "thing" that *can* "go bump in the night"?
Then what is that *sound?—now!—from that shadow! What's that
    sight?*

ALONE

Alone is man's most
bitter situation.
Alone, man has less
than half himself
for company.

How Late I Learned

So many things I did not know:
That skin can itch, and toenails grow,
That love is touch, and fear is false,
And giggle is a kitten's waltz.

How late I learned—(I never dreamt):
Reward of altruism is contempt!

Cry the word, shout the name!
Earless world *hears?*
"Love?"—in a world of *shame?*—
Drowned in Love's *tears?*

Dirge of "Poet"

In this wholesome house of light
sometimes I stay up all night,
held to scratch—(in *"modern"* fashion)—
phrases that speak truth, compassion.

Truth? Compassion? Love and such?
All escape *my* "modern" touch.

A Memory

The little girl said: "I love you. I'd like to kiss you."
Never in my life had I seen her before. She was perhaps five.
She stood straight before me, hands behind her, looking up at
me.
She said, "I'm Dotty. I'm heavy. Mummy says I shouldn't speak
to strange men."
"And she's right," I said. "You shouldn't. Never, never, never!"
"But you're not a strange man," she said. "I love you. I'd like to
kiss you."
So I leaned down and she kissed me. And I kissed her. And she
tasted like a little girl.
Then I went away. I looked back once and waved. And she
waved.
That was more than thirty years ago. I've never seen her since.
But I can still taste her.

An Oddly Wonderful Thing

In Gramercy Park it's an oddly wonderful thing
How, with the winter still snarling at early spring,
Impossible birds appear suddenly and declaim
Their appearance by singing the city to shame.

Strange wild birds with rich voices one hears in the hills
And meadows and marshes—! Well, anyway: I take pills
To keep me in sleep; but pills or not I wake in the spring—
Groggily foggy, God knows!—and listen to these birds sing
In Gramercy Park! It *is* an oddly wonderful thing!

Why do they stop here? The Park is a mere dropping of green.
You'd think, from a skyway, it would seldom-ever be seen!
Of course, they don't stay, these transients: With great musical
    yawning
They bird-bless the neighborhood and leave at second-day's
    dawning.

Why?

Why do I write of death when I have life?
Why do I see darkness when there's light?
Why do I touch Jesus—and hold a knife?—
And watch a dear face—and live in fright?

AFTER

When life is gone
    Let there be
    Ashes of me
To the four winds consigned.
Flesh nor bone
    Bury ye,
    But cast ye free
What I leave behind.
To earth not alone,
    To air, to sea
    Back fling ye me,
Back to my kind.

The hour is late, and I've been thinking:
(Encouraged by a spot of drinking.)
Am I the man who holds his strings,
Or am *I* held by horrid things?
The window's black as coal unlit,
I say, "I do not care a bit!"
But God!—I care, I ask for light,
For something to dispute my fright.
And then—the window gives me day.
And I say, "Fool!"—and drop to pray.

I said to the lady, "My wife is a saint."
She picked at a nose wart, and answered, "She ain't."
I said to her, "Lady—she said you were kind."
She blinked, and she muttered, "Well—all saints are blind."

I Just Can't Grow Up

Prof Grossgutt (a wide lad),
quite fancies his food.
He dines me each decade.
(I can't be—well—rude)

He dined me last some-day,
The time's a bit hazy.
He served a "grown-up" meal.
(Or am I just crazy?)

Bananas and onions
With ice cream and cheese.
And figs, fish and rhubarb
With fried candied-bees.

And well-honeyed oysters
With blueberried crow.
And clam-covered cream pie
With raw escargot.

For dessert, cabbaged falcon
With worms of Peru
immersed in a dressing
of crushed spider—*peugh*!

I really must stop now—
(I just can't grow up.)
I *must* find a good place
to kneel—and throw up.

Not Mocked

Love is mocked?
Even the nasty people
Hope for the scant-imagined
Warmth of it:
Truth-blind, joyless, soul-dead,
Damned they natheless wait
For something on a street
They've never walked.

Question

Abruptly into my life she came
For a moment—then left me flat.
A word, a note, a spoken name,
A smile, a touch, a tiny flame—
Then nothing, nothing, *nothing* the same.
Why do things have to happen like that?

Fatigue's Delusion

She says the day is lovely-bright.
I peek to see the *day* is *night*!
An *hour* ago she said, "Oh, no!"
(I doubt the night will ever go.)

BORED

I'm so damned bored I could spit in the eye
Of a Corsican thug, or lie down and cry
In a stable with goats and pigs to smell
And hammer the walls and groan and yell!

I'm so damned bored that Time is a wall
So cursedly wide and deep and tall
I could leap and climb and dig and crawl
For a mountain's years, and me still so small
And punily, pukily helpless; my pride
Spent on the wall's black, merciless side!

I'm so damned bored I could beat the ceiling
With the flat of my feet! . . . It's a lousy feeling!

PORK-LACED INQUIRY

Now, *what* did that *rag* say? (The play was "The Prawn.")
It praised my performance but—*Yes*! Look, I'll pawn
My *good* chance for stardom if *some*one will tell me—
Now, wait!—he must stay *off*!—not feel me or smell me!—
If *some*one will say what "Variety" meant
By "Note on this actor: '*Sock Limburger Scent*!' "

Ah, Shaw!

He spent *such* a time!—wrote a play!—touching harlots!
And the comedy ventured such nicely-toned scarlets!
But all—well, uh,—*critics* declared that the tone
Of a *classic* success "*must* adhere to the *bone!*"

So he found an old bone and he gnawed it for years,
And he wrote him a "classic" and—blimey!—it appears
He sank for one reason, one reason alone:
His work was as "witty" and "droll" as a "bone"!

No Soap!

I want to write, now—something, anything—
Anything that might be worth the reading.
What a bowel-stopped thing it is to have full pen,
Full urge, full background of experience
And yet sit and sit!—impatience on a pediment
Frowning at—nothing? But wait! There's *Love*, of course,
And—well, Love! Surely there's Love to be scrawled about.
Well, then, *Love*! Love is—well, of course, of course,
Love is—well, good cripes! Love! It's so, *so* much!—
So wonderful, so right, so new, so—so bloody *old*!
Old as that apple in the mouth of short-ribbed Adam!
Old as the scheme of God's design for—for what?
I mean, for what without cliché, redundancy?
Please. Wait. Love has been done and done. I mean, I'm *out*
Of writing Love. The *water's* gone! I mean, no soap!—
I mean, dry soap is so—well—Oh, nuts! I'm *such* a dope!

To Be a Poet

To be a poet is not only to be able to say things beautifully, it is
to be able to think of beautiful things to say.

To be a poet is to cause men to think beyond the limit of the
minds they've lived with.

To be a poet is to bring truth and beauty into the lives of men
who would not have known of this better living without the
poet's work.

To be a poet is to write and so make of love, for men, a thing
to be taken for granted.

To be a poet is to love, all, without stint, without discrimination.

To be a poet is to *live* in love. Without love, blind love, a poet
is a penman.

Such Numbered Ones

We read, and read again, that poetry,
Of all creative arts, stands lonely-high;
That words put down, precise and orderly,
Give best response to man's eternal "why?"

Well, who reads poetry? "Not I!" says chap.
"Don't make me laugh! It bores me stiff, that crap!'

FROST probes his soul, and scribbles to bestow it,
Yet *hesitates* to call himself a "poet"!
Praise God such numbered ones, with small incentive,
Whip words to life!—*compulsively* inventive!

Betrayal Detailed

Ah, "love," *my* "love," you say you spurned
His overtures with words that burned?

But "love," *my* "love," *how* could you *speak*?—
I *felt* your tongue inside his cheek!

If Honestly!

Great balls of Saul! (Pardon.) I'm *much* annoyed
What boots it
What *I* am? Surely work's worth, *if* worthy,
Snatch-roots it
Out of writer's id!—*should* mute the sneer-lip:
"But—he *drinks*!"
Say if you will—yes!—yes, yes, if *honestly*!—
"*It* stinks!"

STATEMENT EMBARRASSING

I have to pee!
It's the tea!
It goes through one—
 or two or three
  when gathered together—
   like something on the run.
The will's no tether:
One *must* or one's undone.
Yes, it's the tea.
I *have* to pee!

JULY IN JANUARY?

To rise a-jump, and waltz across the room
And twist and bend and leer and snap a girdle?
Surely these joys were hedged to grace the bloom
Of youth? . . . And yet The Old One took the hurdle,
And waltzed and bent and leered and snapped;—it's truth!—
And steered the lady to the couch of youth!

But oh, his steering proved the least of all.
She came out irked. And he came out so small.

Flavor of Empty Effort

I am so bitter I taste myself as gall!
Can I be gone from all? Have I shrunk *so* small?
Where is the hour, the day, the *year* I spent
As guiding-*lift* to force of life hell-bent?
There is a doubt that helping ever brings
A lifting out of bad to better things.
But *must* the hand that's gripped the hand of slut
Hang in *always*-memory-taint of smut?

Lament for Love

This is the body's rosy shame:
Breath hot in a stealthy place
And flesh to flesh a dirty game
To give Love an anguished face.

CHILD IN THE PARK

Inside the park a boy-child plays.
Years pass. The boy knows Time and its taint.
Outside the park the "boy" walks and prays
For child in the park: *Himself?—still a saint?*

"COVENTRY"

It's not so nice in "Coventry";
    I've been here twenty years.
I'm stubborn. I still shout for out—
    To nonexistent ears.

RETICENCE

Man reveals his public heart,
    But all the most of him
Hides in a secret second part
    And is the ghost of him.

Alone, Classically

Gramercy! "Now I am alone"—as Hamlet found himself alone.
And how it pleasures *me* to groan and bite the foul-sweet bone
Of *my* disturbances, *my* problems, *my* whisky-sour gripes!—
To moan and bravely fight the phony urge to slice my queasy
    tripes
"With a bare bodkin!"

               So far, so good.

                         But! See!—for *me*, "to be,
"Or not to be" is not at *all* "the question!" Me, I must "*be*"
Or sacrifice the weepy fun of groaning, moaning, biting
On the sweet-foul bone of gripes and problems so delighting
To the sly preoccupation of a this-day silly ass—
Who knows his classic Lincoln, too, so knows, "This, too, will
    pass!"

This Humble Sense

What can I leave? This crip'ling sense benumbs me!
Brahms is sounding; Milton's voice endumbs me.
How in here-this-my-day can *I* scrawl thoughts to last,
When *God*-strain nulls my urge—from a God-led past?

"A" for Effort?

My past is dark, my present, milky,
I *can't* presume my future's silky.

But presents *mine!—here!*—so I'll write
With optimism all the night!

LOVE IN A GROUP

Love in a group knows loneliness more lonely than any other
loneliness.

Love in a group—its loved object gone away, lost, *torn* away—

Desperately, in *scalding* desperation, can't believe (yet knows!)
that many faces

Are as out of knowing, *feeling* of this loneliness as—as squash
impaled on sticks!

Love *can't* believe there is no knowing in the group; no knowing
of the need

For closeness, for the flesh touch of that Love that *lived* in Love
only for *this* Love.

That closeness! This Love knew it! (Damn the group! Squash
heads! Blind!)

Close . . . *our* Love . . . *us!*—less lonely than the joined together
tongue and groove

Of master woodwork. Less lonely than my eager lips—on live-
willing yours.

OF UNBORN SOUL

The man who throws a fellow man to dogs and desperation
Is building, for his "house of hope," a dwelling of damnation.
With seeming-human intellect, this man of of unborn soul,
Will plan for afterlife and earn—a moldy, earth-walled hole.

ALONG THAT PATH

What a question! "Guardian Angels?" You ask, "*Are* there
Guardian Angels?"
Oh, my Lovely, Stately, Lately-sinning, Sinned-against!—of
course there are!
Did no one tell you?—(Are you *sure*?)—tell you when to look,
and where to look—
To see *yours*? . . . So?—you disremember? Then lean close—*close*!
—your ear to my mouth.

There. My darling, someone told you; yes, he did!—there, to-
gether on that bench,
Your hand in his, he told you—of your Guardian Angel: that he
lived in *you*.
In faith you found in something, *someone*!—faith that gave *him*
stature,
Substance, flesh, to fill your eyes, to take your hand, to guide
your pretty feet
Along *that* path, (where you moved always, always finely as
a ripple might)
Most surely, *cara*, to the splendid place where you belong, and
must be!

Yes, he told you, darling: "The mirror on the cabinet?—or wall,
Or any place?" (Remember now?) "You believing, seeing then,
Yes, quite *touching* what your heart will know to be the very
   body
Of a living love?—you standing, looking at the one that's you,
The one that, being you, is part of one that's part of you,
Of that one just behind you, at your side, within, above, before
you?—"

You remember? There, of course you do!—and did and will for
   life! Yes?
And you'll possess the faith in you and him, the faith he needs,
   to *be*!
You will, my Lovely, Stately, No-more sinning, No-more sinned-
   against!—
Or there's no "balm in Gilead"—and *I* know there *is*! I've used it!

For Unforgivables

This is the heart's full knowing
    Of all that is not right:
The muted, hopeless crying
    Of a distant child at night.

The Weather Was Against

I so liked the newfound friend who came to tea today.
(The weather was against all liking:—cold-wet and gray.)
But she, the freckle-honest, mother-lovely person,
Gave the house, room, corner—all the property!—and, yes, gave
    me
A dark-eyed, golden-humored, sweet-limbed guarantee
That nothing—whether weather or we-all or here—would worsten
While all-of-here, and all of us, would cherish memory of this
    person.

HILL FIELD

We have a hill field that looks down on a valley.
(Up the lane and through the gap; turn to the left a bit.)
It's cold now, and still; winter has it till tomorrow.
Then sun will warm it, home-come bird call to bird,
Creature sound his creaky pipe in new-green fragrance!

And we will go to it, lie on it, and feel its life
Friendly-firm, enfolding, beneath our backs; *taking* the sun.
And when we do that we'll know again that in *this* life
We've found a place that lives beyond our breathing,
A place to *meet* beyond this breath, beyond this life;
This place, our home hill, our field of meeting, of returning.

TWELVE TO SEVEN

She loves her God, her man and her cat.
She loves them thus, in the order that
You read them here. And it's twelve to seven
This love will see all of them walking Heaven!

OTHER POEMS

CHURCHILL

With his stick he pointed
    at the bird
That lay dead on the path
    in front of him.
He wept. It is known that,
    speechless; he wept.

God love this greatest
    of our men
Who found room in his heart
    for compassion.

Man's weak. Only weakness forms and feeds
the scabby roots of human error:
Lust, greed, and hate, and cruelty—
silly pomp, false pride, and vanity—
envy, jealousy and sour gossip—
sick reach, and ruthless snatch, and parsimony—
self-doubt, and cowardly timidity—

These are the poisoned-feeble stems of plant.

GIVE

The hour of living should have little to do
        with the time of living.
The hour of giving should have less, much less
        than the time of giving.
How many walk past the outstretched hand, the
        mystery of the mendicant:
How many walk past the hour of life that—
        (oh, they don't know it!) is their last—
So—if the "poor one" asks you—give!
So may your hour be judged by that last hour!—
        think!—and *give!*

Never call a man your "Friend"
Till you've reached a desperate end.
If he's waiting there, concerned,
You've a "Friend"—you *must* have earned!

152

LINCOLN

He lived so short a time ago,
And we seem so far away from him.
We see him in bronze, feel we know him
From the words he spoke, from his written words,
We laud him from the written words as master
Of English prose. (All the world lauds him!)
But oh! the meaning and purpose of his words:
Did they die with him?—die with the heart that stopped?—
Die with the heart and mind that surely did live
On the beat and breath of one song, *one* song?—
Compassion?

SIX-FEET-TWO IN NORTH AMERICA

Most of me is so far from the ground
That, if I fell, struck by my own blood
Or the dead weight of a quiet heart,
The "czar" in China might hear the sound,
Look up ("up" would be "down") and take the thud
To mind as the devil's ribald fart
At nonsense: Rice from the blood of men,
Mindless wisdom, death for "why?" or "when?"
Peace through hate, compassion's breath in sharks,
Chained freedom, a wanton Chinese Marx!
The "czar" *might* take to mind my fleshy wallop.
(God's Virgin Mother *might* have been a trollop.)

I KNOW A BLIND MOHAMMEDAN

Who is more worthy than Lonz, the monk, who tries
To place his ears and nose and tongue and eyes
In and on the heads of thousand Christian Neighbors
By Christian pouring-out of strong sermonic labors?

Who is more worthy? Lonz, the monk, has never wasted
Smell or sound or sight of Book, has deeply *tasted*
Bible lore beyond light-shallow taking of that Book,
Has *soul*-absorbed, by stare-gaze infinite!—not just a look!

Oh, I do revere this Lonz, the monk! He *lives* for God!
And God will lift and take his soul-form from the sod!
Yes, this I know! I've seen him comfort many, many;
And never has he frightened child or "child"—not any!

But, but, and but again, and yet again,
I know a blind Mohammedan who lives in panic.
He's casual—speaks of Allah as "Good 'Seven-Eleven'."
Yet, by his speaking, I believe Love *is* of Heaven.

ALONE

You're stupid? You're limited?
But surely you're not the *most*
Stupid or limited.
You cry? You're afraid?
But surely you don't cry alone,
Or crouch sick, *alone* in fear.
You work—drive life-dulled mind
To scrawl *that* word, *right* word?
But surely others do and do—
And end the piece in doubt of merit,
And live endlessly in that doubt,
No world's voice that *rates* the word.

Believe!—you've warming company
In misery and loneliness.
Believe!—unconsciously great others
Send you understanding greetings,
Offer hands in friendly-loving
Gesture naming hope, and strength—
Fulfillment and its peace—for you.

If I Ask

If I ask for proper, for adequate, reward for work I have turned
out,
If I ask for no more than acknowledgment that my hand, this
hand
Was the father, the sole dedicated parent of my *own* work—
If I ask that this ego-necessary credit be given me before I'm
dead, my life burned out—
Well—if I ask this—being a high-proud but honest man—is this
demand
The one of a high-proud man, or the one of a contemptible char-
latan, a crud, a phony jerk?

A Statement

You ask for communicable reason that
I should have so deeply adored a cat?
Pah! I did, and I do, and continue to
In grief and compassion and love.
And that's that!

LESSON IN FACT
"Moral"

Give, forgive and give. The "moral":
"Giving breeds an inner quarrel."
Heart ends giving Mind its head.
Mind puts silly Heart to bed.

Story

Fell gave a friendly smile to lonely Jack.
Jack's January lips were set in sorrow.
He shivered, made no try to pay Fell back.
Fell hopes he will—today—perhaps tomorrow.

Fell gave himself to certain lovely one.
In "love" (she called it that) she spoke a name.
Fell's name was "Fell"—or "Dear." She called him "Jon"—
Then laughed and lied. And *Fell* it was felt shame.

Fell gently gave his voice to "Prostie" Belle.
She, snarling, told him he should "go to hell!"
He thinks when Belle is gladly through with dying
She won't go there, not Belle. . . . He saw her crying.

Fact

"Mind puts silly Heart to bed?"
"Heart gives mighty Mind its head?"
Pooh! The Heart that yields to Mind
Dwells content in Mind's behind!

Friendship

Friendship is emotion, hung
on a slack, frayed string.
Time pulls the string.
Either end can hold two
who have the gift of love.
Without burden of any
gift of love
the string will break and dangle impotently,
and fall and rot—
unburdened—
the empty part of
silly chance.

Futility?

I strike the paper with my pen—
And strike again—again—and then, when
Stupid words occur, I go to bed—
And wish, dear God, that I were dead!

But!—next day I try again—and—*oh!*—
I write a decent piece! What *ho!*

Ah, me, I would a hero be,
and here I sit in apathy.
(And "apathy's" a sticky stool
that weds the bottom of a fool.)

INTERRUPTION

The supreme insult is interruption:

He—She barks, "Your words are empty nonsense!
Your mouthings echo from a vacant head!
Please turn off the tap of silly lingo!
Please! Shut up! *I* speak! *You* are a balmy fool!"

The God of all insult is interruption.

COMMON SENSE SAYS

Where is the man who all-willingly works?
Ask him—he'll tell you that work is for jerks.
Common sense says we should all sit like slobs
and watch while the other guy muscles the jobs.
Common sense, then, says: "Let's all think the same,
And all starve together, with no one to blame."

"NELLIE'S GARTER"*

By drowsy-bed gentled, an odd tale I've mentaled.
Make me an offer; I'll barter.
These fore-written deals have great bargain appeals.
Consider a trade on "Nell's Garter."

For sure, when I wake, (and I *will* for *your* sake!)
"Nell's Garter" will be here to swap.
I'll take a thing broken, to serve as a token
Of what may be left in your shop.

You see, "Nellie's Garter"—(the trull *was* a martyr)
Could do as a trussified savior
For object that's stopping or brokenly flopping:
A heart, say?—in anguished behavior?

---

*Nell Gwyn, of course.

ALONE

She's alone, quite all alone and so pitiful.
She's ugly—with the ugliness of timeless loneliness
That clouds the once bright-velvet lighting of her eyes,
That drapes the early satin fabric of her flesh
With tired crepe. Look! The crinkly sag-brown pockets
Hang from below those eyes like small dead mice!

She's all alone—lives, walks alone, her back, bone-warped,
Mounded, fat-seeming: vile, incongruous burden
On her wasted stick-thin form, her tottering body.
Her gray hands, like the feet of an unclean bird,
Shaking, move painfully but constantly and tenaciously
To seize at nothing, to grip the nothing—and drop it.
She's all alone. She'll tell you why; she talks nothing else:
"I took love. Love? Yes, I took love. Oh, I took such love!—
And made a thing of it, a silken thing to blow my nose upon!
I took love, *took it! Cleaned my boots with it!* . . . And it left me."

WEATHER

Not a stir of air, not a breath of breeze;
Leaves lie dead as a hangman's holiday.
I?—last November?—complained of a sneeze?
(A sneeze would be something to boast of today.)
But bless all!—today we complain of the heat,
Tomorrow we'll wheezily snort and complain
Of the cold that explodes into arthritic pain—
But think, *please!—does* God *plan* for his children's defeat?

WHAT WOULD YOU DO?

What would you do if God had made for you
A pathway through a darkened wood—
Tall, sky-crowned trees whose green and rustling leaves
Were parted by a gentle breeze,
To let the golden lances of the sun
Lighten groups of blood-red flowers
Upspringing from a bed of velvet moss—
Earth's flesh of green, gold-pierced and bleeding—
What would you do and fate had made you blind?

I sailed a kite on a black-dark night,
and found the emptiness of sight.
I felt the string like a living thing—
and learned that sightless life holds fright.

Shut your mind,
Blank out all there is of thought,
Only in God's blackness
Can price of mind be bought!

PRAYER

Miles are the distance from here to there.
Here is this county;
there is anywhere.
Here is ill prospect, black-shadowed and bare.
There is light's bounty
and—*What-do-I-care!*

Miles, God, are the distance from darkness to light!
God!—sharp-wrench this county sun high from this night!

Day is the light that breaks out of night.
Night is the darkness that robs light of sight.
Light, sight and living are one with the sun
But God!—death and darkness are surely not one!

Josephine!*

Not quite right in form
Yet dearly far from wrong:
Now New Life has touched you—
Great eyes and lovely head,
And sweetly comic body—
And called the all of them
Immeasurably more
Than food of laughter.

Our Little "Doc"

We have had, among some friends,
Our little "Doc"—the little "Hen."
She was there to mesh our ragged ends.
She was there always, always when
Most we needed her—she was always there—
Always, always. She might have said, "I care."
She helped us, healed us. Her hand
Brought peace. She might have said, "I understand."
She always said—she'd *order:* "Go to bed,
And take this funny nothing for your head."
And we would go to bed and take the funny pill.
And wake up without any form of ill.

So now, dear God, we pray our little friend
Will always find beginning at the end.

*To Josephine Hull.

164

SHASTA

I've heard tell from long-winded roll-gaited guys,
Big brine stinking fellows with salt in their eyes,
That oceans and seas and lakes of good size
Represent all the beauty and charm 'neath the skies.

But I've seen the ocean and I've sailed the sea,
And damned if I know where their beauty can be,
Blue-green nervous water monotonously
Swishing a cold smelly wetness 'neath me.

Oh I love lofty places, and small wonder why,
For the beauties that hit me are quiet and dry,
They run not to depths but reach up for the sky,
And their songs are a peaceful whispering sigh.

To the fish with your oceans, the mountains are mine,
I looked upon Shasta today, and the wine
Of its calm, breathless beauty ajiggled my spine—
Christ's chosen cathedral, its summit His shrine.

WORDS TO EDNA ST. V. M.

My candle does not burn at all.
It has no wick.
And oh, my friend, the hours crawl
Through darkness thick!

I Could Be an R.C. Else

"Confession" is to empty one of sin
By word of agile tongue and heart and mind?
I'm so designed
that tongue and mind
quite fail to start
the draining of my heart
of sin—a single sin—a small, ill-hidden sin.

I pray, I pray
for something gay
to pass ill time away.

"Wisdom"—The Word

A wise man said, "But no one!—*no!*—shoots Santa Claus!"
And wise men *wisely* name our tight beliefs and laws.
But Santa Claus is Love, indeed is God, is Christ.
and *is* this Proper Trinity, by *all* men, priced above the lure of
  execution?

Dog Eats Dog

Man lives *not*
   by bread alone?
Not!
He keeps his life
   by use of knife
     in strife—
And sucks a bone!

In All Modesty

Let's talk:
The right to walk upon the water
Is one that really shouldn't oughter
Be the right of *common* men.
And yet, I meet so *many* when
I walk!

Necessity for Second Thought

I'm slightly puzzled. See: just now
I *thanked* a lady with a bow.
She answered sweetly, pleasantly:
"You're much obliged," she said to me.
I may be wrong; I'm not so bright.
But something there seems not quite right.

Eavesdroppings

She said it! I heard it! We sat side by side:
"There's *some* people rarely commit suicide."
Her eyes were all-knowing, her brow high and wide.
(We rode on a bus.) And I tried to decide
Just who was the fool—when she said on that ride:
"There's *some* people rarely commit suicide!"

Ice!—it's a blessing!—
So coldly nice!
But used for drinks.
It waters twice!

She told me, that teacher in small-lower grade,
"Your heart holds your finger, your heart is afraid."
So I've counseled my finger to govern my heart,
And now, at the end, I have horse behind cart.

"Nothings"?

It's night, and the window's as black as tar.
Beyond is the place where the "Nothings" are.
And yet I'm sure, if I stepped outside,
The "Nothings" would scamper away and hide.

Frustration in Moronia

We met in a "Rest Home."
  (I thought she was dead.
She just made a practice
   Of losing her head.)

We courted for weeks
   'Neath a Mealy-Bug tree.
She said she loved her,
   And I swore I loved me.

Oh, our love was so different,
   So far from the norm.
We both felt that puling
   Was simply good form.

It all seemed so balanced,
   So lucid and true.
(Both knowing that *one*
   Could live cheaply as two.)

And so we decided
   To "throw in our lot,"
To sort of co-mingle
   Our prunes in one pot.

And we might have, you know,
   In a different place.
But on Old Liver Hill
   There was not enough space.

For she was a female
   And I am a male.

And Dr. Immune said,
  "So sorry! No sale!"

But oft, as I long for
  Just *someone* to blame,
I can't help but wonder:
  Now, what *was* her name?

KILMER SAID

Kilmer said he'd never see
"A poem lovely as a tree."
But me, because I try to grow'm,
I see a tree as quite a *poem*.

"IF" AGAIN

If water were not so wet, a man could drown himself in com-
fort—if he thought well of the idea.

If cold steel were not so painful in the flesh—more like a sliver
of stiff old cheese—a man could cut his throat merrily!

If rope were more elastic, and less rough to the touch, a man
could hang himself, the while reflecting upon the good fortune
of such a happy-weathered day for the job.

If death were not so deadly, a man could—but it *is!*

"Raveled Sleeve"

You are observed?—policed?—peeked at? You are frowned
Upon by all that has a kinship with the ground?
Windowed buildings check you? Empty *fields* observe
Your jerky step and gesture? Bare walls serve
To spy upon the fevered working of your mind?
Winds touch your wrist inquisitively and find
A racing *terror?* . . . Stop, now; weep if it helps, weep.
You're far from mad, not mad at all. You just need sleep.

Upon Sitting Down to Attempt the Writing of a Poem

Sitting here, waiting, still; lax-browed felicity
Giving me urge and skill for word simplicity:
Why do I toss, flip, flick away that urge, and tool
Into the dreary, bony lap of last year's fool?—
Who'd snidely fox me into aping what he teaches:
Yesterday's "abstract" inanity! For ink? "Use laundry bleaches!"

ONLY MAN!

You inch, inch to the line of righteousness
With fear, fear that you'll be challenged.
What are you? Just and only *man!*
So you must, over this hurdle,
Claim anything you can!—
You!—weak and only *man!*

WORDS WITH A MOUNTAIN

The mountain says, "You're a narrow thing, and short,
A runt, a three-score breath, less than a maggot's wart!"
Must I say "yes, yes I'm *nothing*" to the mountain?
What *can* "a narrow thing, and short" say to a mountain?
Anything? Yes! It *can* and *does* say: "Do tell!
God's 'runt'? His 'three-score breath' holds all there is of *hell!*"

As a Voter

Just why does a senator, powered by votes,
Poo-phooey his voters as bunny-brained goats?
For sure he must think of their thinking as slack:
They vote him in "blue" and he legislates "black"!

They tell me the senate's a "gentleman's club,"
Exclusive and cushy and—well, a *gent's* pub!—
Where *much* costs you little, and *little* is splendid!
But cripes! Without votes all the splendor is ended!

So what in the hell is the matter wtih *us*?—
The diddle-brained us-es who vote for "Old Gus"?
We *want* to keep "Gus" in the gravy and cream?—
The *better* to boogle us? Moses! I'll scream!

I voted for "Gus" 'cause he right-outly said
He'd pension us all at a million a head!
Well, I *don't* want to start inner-party dissension,
But *where* is my tax-exempt, "Gus"-labeled pension?

God made the world
And then He found that it was earthy,
No part of Heaven was there.
And so He gave unto an Angel His command,
And sent to grow close to the heart of man
A rose, from His own garden,
That man might smell its freshness,
Breathe its breath, and know
That part of Heaven was his own to cherish.

A Shoelace, A Shophar

Life *sells!* Buy a funeral? *From* someone! A thought?—
A shoelace, a shophar? What need is not bought?
And "buyer" grants "seller," prenatally taught.

Donkeys sell labor for hay; cows their milk.
Horses sell "blood," speed, their bearing of "silk.'
Cannibal gentlemen peddle their ilk!

Gamblers sell roosters they market as "cocks."
Statesmen sell whiskey by taxing the crocks.
Bawds will unfailingly charge you for pox!

Life sells of the *all* of life, all has a sale.
Maiden asks marriage, and Great Ghost!—*our* male
At cost of his face will penistically fail!

Fox, ostrich and elephant, beetle and worm
Sell, peddle and barter. (A *goat* offers sperm!)
Each least of them carries eternity's germ.

For certain, Great Ghost set the live on the earth
To sell!—for their being, their pleasure, their mirth,
And sorrow, too, sorrow—to death-end, from birth.

CURRENT ANSWER TO AN OLD QUESTION

"My son, my son, what hast thou done
   To be sent to Botany Bay?"
Ah, mummy, I bashed a saucy one
   That snooped and got in me way!

Mindin' me business I was, y'see,
   Yes, out on a piddlin' job.
Shillin's, no more, was the worth to me
   Of a wee little shop to rob.

(The *granny* was old and smelled of dread.
   I did her a favor to cosh *her* head.)

But mummy, the tart was the grief:
   A customer, in for a packet.
It's *wrong* for the sight of a thief
   To cause such a *screamin'* racket!

I paused to molest her. I shouldn't have done.
   (The feel of her blood spoiled me day.)
And that's all, me mummy, that I have done
   To be sent to "Botany Bay."

GENTLES

Gentles I've known are *well* known as "splendid."
Odd. For they're *not* so, or reality's ended:
Partly they're smarmy and partly—well, *mean*!
Witness the sliver of steel in my spleen!

Gentles I've known are "men who will help."
Odd. For they *feed* on the lately-come whelp:
Mentally cannibalistically greedy,
Slyly consuming the lately-come needy.

Gentles I've known are highly respected,
Stooped by the medals their "worth" has collected.
Odd! For a pig would deny them the sty!
Gentles who bargain an aye for an eye!

"AS A RING OF GOLD—"

Now, after so long, you say you want to speak the truth?—
That now, at last, you know the "need" of truth?—its "wisdom"?—
The need to feel its "beauty" part of you?—to "live" it?
After so long, now, you "might as well be dead as such a fraud?"

But how pitiful!—how horrible!—(if what you say is true)—
Now to give *all* truth!—and see it met by deathless disbelief!

PETITON

So many of them, so million many;
Dear people with their hearts open,
Primed, hungry for the love they want—
Fill them, Love! Love, give them the treasure
Of You!—You from another heart!

UNHOUSEWORTHY

Why must it be held that the *hour* of writing
Makes worst or best of the quality of writing?
Dear people scold me from "the pen" when time says "no!"
"Jeeks!" I howl, bald-eyed, nasty-lipped. "Go, *do* go! Blow!"

Oh, Patience, *great!—I* know!—here's un*house*worthy man!
But *bog* me!—I *must* write my writing when I can!

PREJUDICE

Who fools
with mules
will rule out
stools.

God Forbid It Should Happen!

Acquaint
a saint
with taint:
He ain't!

Lament of a Steer

My amusion: indolence—
just lying.
My confusion: impotence—
and dying!

Irrefutable Statement in Brief

Fire, the sire
Of all man's desire!

Lament for Compassion

This is the heart's full knowing
Of all that is not right:
The muted, hopeless crying
Of an unknown child at night.

ADVICE

If music is for talking,
Kindly go a-walking.

If music is for listen-to,
Stay—or we'll be missin' you.

UNWRITTEN COMMANDMENT

All living things are born to kill.
All things living must kill or die.
Murder!—the plan of Original Will!—
Unwritten commandment! . . . I wonder why.

TOOTH IS NOT STRONGER THAN FRICTION

Philosophic let us be,
Grunting here in agony.
Nothing worsens worse than worst.
Toothache *snubs* atomic burst!

My Complaint

He said his mind was "a bowl of worms."
    He'd killed a "Sunday Saint."
Noted psychiatrists mumbled terms.
    He's hanged! . . . That's my complaint.

Lines to the Friend of a Little Dead Boy-killed Boy

Ah, little boy, if you must die,
Then die *when* you belong to die:
Some distant day, at ten times seven,
Not now, please, when you're just eleven.

Ah, little boy, if you must die,
Then die *where* you belong to die:
Not like your friend there, in the street,
Carved up like a piece of meat!

LINES TO THE MEMORY OF ANGELO POPO

See the *soul*-dead steal into good Angelo's digs!
(He's alive when they enter, the poison-boweled pigs!)
So!—they *kick* him to steal less than coffee-and-cakes!—
Yes, kick him! Then *stick* him!—the merciless *snakes!*
So he dies like a shoat as he bleeds from the throat
Like anything! . . . Ah, *good* brother Popo!—you're dead!
But the good *rest* with good. Friend—*your* Friend also bled.

THE OLDING, IN THE NAME OF

How little sympathy is offered to creeping dissolution,
The inevitable slow failure of body and mind.
What compassion is held for the inchmeal execution
Of the creative glow that wants to live to *give*?—the glow
  designed
Divinely as perpetuation bait; its dull-to-gay-to-antic
Physical accomplishments: by gauging eye the responsive hand
A-grubbing, healing, tossing rice; *all* body in hotly frantic
Indulgence; this, these and all, the voice of human demand
To express, to continue, to empty itself, to fulfill
Urges that seem to lie out of the mind, that do lie *in* the mind—
Consider!—urges, demands, that must, that will, always *will*
Die, die, die!—that *must* discontinue and leave a rotting rind,
A foul shell of what was a potent human body and mind! . . .
Give sympathy for creeping impotence! Give warm glance, give
  eyelight!
Or *trade* them: kindness to the olding!—for kindness in *your*
  twilight.

Cock of the "Captain's Walk"

The wind is from the south.
"Doodle," the golden rooster on the roof peak,
Vanes the weather for me. Of course, I *could* seek,
Myself, with moistened finger, for the trend of blow.
But spare my spittle! One glance at "Doodle" and I know
The wind is from the south.

The Angry Bee

The angry bee can hardly see
    For rage at human being.
But clever thing, he still can sting,
    So what cares he for seeing?

The angry lout can see, and shout
    At stingless bee . . . departed.
(But turn the page and cancel rage.)
    The bee and he have parted.

There's Past Eternity

Howl shame upon the one who *does* know better.
Weep pity for the one not born to see.
The palace brat?—whose "blood" demands a debtor?
The gutter snipe?—who's never seen a tree?

Ha! *Both* never *born?* In past eternity
What *fed* this mindless, *antic* urge to *be?*

Companions in Weariness

I have a headache, I can't write more.
I'm now quite like the exhausted whore.
We both, no doubt, utter similar prayers:
We just can't, again, climb those Goddamned stairs!

My rhyme has left me and her rhythm's dead.
She's worn in thigh and I in my head.
(At least, she contends that her legs are in trouble,
And me, from my neck to my scalp I've gone double.)

So let us collapse and retire, eh, dearie?
Your can is so flat and my brow is so weary!

STRIKE OFF HIS NAME

Ah, the poor sick Pantheon cats, so lost,
Tossed to the mercies of anyone's whim!
Give *naught* for *naught*, God!—and to *him* the *most*
For his fleetingest pity for kitty! To him
Of nothing of slightest compassion for cat,
Give him a blow of catastrophe's fist,
Diet of bone worms and putrified rat!
Strike off his name from the life-worthy list!

DOES IT MATTER?

Now, if you, my friend, were born and raised
Like a dockyard dolt, would you be fazed
By the need to meet and eat with a prince?
Not I! I was bold! But I've wondered since:

Was he kind? Did he pity? Or did he *believe*
The me who believed that I *had* to deceive?

Lines in Defense of the Feeding of Birds

How can you say, you pinch-eyed yellow-blood,
That bird is just a feather-lifted bone?
It's plain you've never felt one light upon your finger
In trust—because you patient-loving gained the trust!
I hear you, man of "man": "Cash, money for their frigid six-
    month's feeding?"
Look, frog-soul, let *me* say: *You* are a *lack-brain*!
And I would be obliged if you would cease to linger
In this neighborhood!—the dying yellow of your dust
In distance would delight me! . . . Pooh! *I* am absurd?—
Beyond *myself* I prize the breathing of a bird?
Well, neighbor, I'll hug my "corny, sentimental" place!
You take your way of living life—and *pant* for grace!

YOUR HAND, YOUR WILL

There have been several times, my "friend," when I'd have
    snuffed my life
Had I not had your hand to hold, your will to fasten to mine.
I've grown so goddamned sick-in-the-gut with the hog-tied strife
Forced upon a nature not made for fun in fighting! *Fun?* The
    design
Wrought by *someone's* work upon a flesh like mine says to that
    flesh,
"Fight, slob, for the shame of running! Fight though you puke
    in fright!"

God a'mercy!—mercy?—are You mercy?—You who cynically mesh
Your will with the backward bowels of my-this weakness?—
    You, *All* of *Right?*

See, "friend": I still inhale!—not through some archly determined
    will!
I still inhale because *you* give me breath! Because you love me
    still!

Do Drop in About Five!

The chattering, the nattering,
The talk without a smattering
Of thought behind it—

The snickering, the likkering,
The sound of tiddly bickering:
I do *so* mind it.

The pasted grin upon my chin,
The sweaty social trap I'm in:
Sure hell designed it!

Cogg's "Face"

Now, if you, my friend, were born and raised
Like a dockyard dolt, would you be fazed
By the need to meet and eat with a prince?
Not Cogg! He was bold! But he's wondered since:
That prince—did he pity? Or did he *believe*
The Cogg who believed that he *had* to deceive?

All around the valley, and back along the path
that leads to home and friend and love—
Weary-legged and sweating and a trifle sick,
And oh, so glad to have the duty done of walking
for the sake of recommended exercise—
How fine for health!

And on the last wee hill the legs—no mind to power-loss grow
    quick
To close the gap between the stupid little hill and arms, those
    lovely arms,
that welcome, praise and squeeze in laughed assurance of pure
    love—
How fine for living!